WHEN MOTOR RACING WAS FUN

Ken Tyrrell with the author in the Tyrrell motor home at Silverstone in 1994.

WHEN MOTOR RACING WAS FUN

Tales of Classic Years on the Track

Foreword by Sir Stirling Moss OBE

BRYAN APPS

HALSGROVE

First published in Great Britain in 2009

British Library Cataloguing-in-Publication Data
A CIP record for this title is available from the British Library

ISBN 978 1 84114 966 0

HALSGROVE
Halsgrove House,
Ryelands Industrial Estate,
Bagley Road, Wellington, Somerset TA21 9PZ
Tel: 01823 653777   Fax: 01823 216796
email: sales@halsgrove.com

Part of the Halsgrove group of companies
Information on all Halsgrove titles is available at: www.halsgrove.com

Printed and bound in China by SNP Leefung Printers Ltd

CONTENTS

To my wife, Kathleen
and our children,
Richard, Wendy and Michael

BIBLIOGRAPHY

The author has sought information from a number of published sources and gratefully acknowledges the authors and publishers of the following works in particular: *Ayrton Senna* by Christopher Hilton; *Nigel Mansell* by Nigel Mansell and Derick Allsop; *Beyond the Limit* by Professor Sid Watkins; *Winners* edited by Brian Laban; *Winning Is Not Enough* by Jackie Stewart; *Behind the Scenes* by Louis T Stanley; *Vignettes and Memories* by Louis T Stanley; *Grand Prix* by Trevor R Griffiths; *The Chequered Flag* by Ivan Rendall; *The History of Motor Racing* by William Boddy and Brian Laban; *Hitler's Grands Prix in England* by Christopher Hilton; *Goodwood – A Private View* by Cyril Read and Robin Read; *B.R.M.* by Raymond Mays and Peter Roberts; *B.R.M. – The Saga of British Racing Motors* by Doug Nye with Tony Rudd; *Fifty Famous Motor Races* by Alan Henry; *One Hundred Years of Motoring* by Raymond Flower and Michael Wynn Jones; *John Cooper Grand Prix Carpet-Bagger* by John Cooper with John Bentley; *Cooper Cars* by Doug Nye; *Enzo Ferrari* by Gino Rancati; *Ferrari: the Grand Prix Cars* by Alan Henry; *Ferrari* by Hans Tanner and Doug Nye; *Famous Racing Cars* by Doug Nye; *The Formula One Years* by Timothy Collings and Sarah Edworthy; *Formula 1: 1950–Today* by Rainer W Schlegelmilch and Hartmut Lehbrink; *Stirling Moss* by Robert Edwards; *Stirling Moss: The Champion without a Crown* by Pierre Menard and Jacques Vassal; *Stirling Moss: My Cars, My Career* by Stirling Moss with Doug Nye; *Formula One* by David Tremayne and Mark Hughes; *Track Pass* by Geoff Goddard; *Maserati* by Richard Crump and Rob de la Rive Box; *Grand Prix!* by Mike Lang; *The Power and the Glory* by Ivan Rendall; *Grand Prix Yesterday and Today* by Bruce Jones; *A History of the World's Racing Cars* by Richard Hough and Michael Frostick; *Brooklands* by G. N. Georgano; *A History of Brooklands Motor Course* by William Boddy; *Classic Racing Cars* by Doug Nye and Geoff Goddard; *Great Cars, Sports and Racing* by Doug Nye; *British Cars at Le Mans* by Rominique Pascal; *The Art of Gordon Crosby* by Peter Garnier; *Goodwood* by Peter Garnier; *Mon Ami Mate* by Chris Nixon; *50 Years of the Formula One World Championship* edited by Bruce Jones; *The Golden Age of Motor Racing* by Tim Hill; *Motor Racing the Golden Age* by John Tennant; *Formula One Unseen Archives* by Tim Hill; *The Automotive Book* by Ralph Stein; *The Monaco Grand Prix* by Alex Rollo; *Monaco Grand Prix, Portrait of a Pageant* by Craig Brown and Len Newman; *Formula One Through the Lens* by Nigel Snowdon; *Autocourse Grand Prix Annuals* by Hazleton; *Grand Prix Heroes* by William Ensor; *The British Racing Hero* by Derick Allsop; *Murray Walker's Formula One Heroes* by Murray Walker and Simon Taylor; *The Grand Prix Drivers* edited by Steve Small; *The Jaguar Challenge* by Ken Wells; *Touch Wood!* by Duncan Hamilton; *My Two Lives* by Rene Dreyfus with Beverly Rae Kimes; *The History of English Racing Automobiles* by David Weguelin; *Piloti, Che Gente* by Enzo Ferrari; *British Motor Cars 1950-51* edited by A. H. Lukins; *Racing the Silver Arrows* by Chris Nixon; *Mercedes Benz Grand Prix Racing 1934–1955* by George C Monkhouse. Thanks are due to Ted Gee who photographed all the paintings for publication.

FOREWORD BY
SIR STIRLING MOSS OBE

SEPTEMBER 18th 1948 was important for me as at Goodwood on that day I drove in the first ever race in the UK since the War and won it in a Cooper 500.

Unbeknown to me the following Easter Monday was important for a twelve year old called Bryan, later to become the Reverend Bryan Apps, and one of a rare brand of dog-collared enthusiasts, because at Goodwood on that day he attended his first race meeting as a spectator. He is a vicar who became hooked on motor racing.

When his bishop invited him to serve the pastoral needs of the new estates of Andover in the 1960s he bought a double-decker bus, which the national newspapers called 'the world's first mobile church'.

Not long afterwards, when the bishop asked him to raise money for the Church Urban Fund, our hero, using his God-given persuasive manner, responded by establishing world records with a Hornby train and a Scalextric car, helped by members of his Church, I.B.M. and *The Guinness Book of Records*.

Bryan was really hooked, and went to every Goodwood meeting, except 1962. He chose that day to marry Kath at St Peter's in Carmarthen. His big day was also a big day for me. In his case, it was the start of a happy union and the sharing of his life. In mine, it meant leaving a sport I loved and meant that I had to start working for a living!

Due to Bryan's patriotism, he became an ardent B.R.M. supporter. This allowed him to forge a lasting friendship with Raymond Mays, the father of the project. This book covers this association in some detail, together with his proposal to publish his B.R.M. scrapbooks in 1985.

The latter led to a long friendship with Ken and Norah Tyrrell, and he was a frequent guest in their pits and motor home until the team was sold to B.A.R.

Bryan took up painting as a hobby when he was forty-five, and was surprised to find that he was able to sell the results of his work. In the years that followed, he has given away over 200 of his motor sport pictures to a large number of people who are well known in our sport. These include Enzo Ferrari himself. I am also one of the lucky recipients.

This book gives the reader the chance to see them but, more than that, there are many nuggets to be mined from the books he has read and the letters he received from those on the inside, and it is a reminder of those days which I enjoyed 'When Motor Racing was Fun'.

Sir Stirling Moss OBE
2009

WHEN MOTOR RACING WAS FUN

NO MOTOR RACE could ever be dull. Murray Walker said it and I believe it to be true. But I like to recall the days when motor racing was fun. When money was seen as the means of racing rather than its object; when winners drank their champagne instead of spraying it over others; when racing cars looked like cars and were painted in their national colours; when racing drivers could be clearly seen in their open cockpits clad in leather helmets and goggles, and when anyone with £500 could buy a Cooper 500 and go motor racing.

Enjoying the chase, Baron Toulo de Graffenried in his 2-litre Maserati in 1953. Inset is from a drawing by Gordon Horner.

The dangers

Of course we are profoundly thankful that, due to the work of Jackie Stewart, Louis Stanley and others, motor racing has become infinitely safer than it was in earlier days. Had the standards of safety not been vastly improved motor racing would surely have been banned by all the authorities long ago. With the loss of so many talented young men like Dick Seaman, Peter Collins and Jim Clark and a number of spectators too, everyone who followed the Sport must have begun to consider, as I did, whether it ought to be continued at the cost of so many lives.

I remember in 1969 offering Henri Pescarola an encouraging smile as he set off from the paddock at Thruxton in his Formula Two Matra. He looked so vulnerable, trapped by his seat belts in the most fragile of cars, and I literally prayed that he would make it safely back again.

Innes Ireland

Yet when Innes Ireland once wrote to me about all the lives that had been lost through motor racing he said this:

> *"I agree with your views on current Grand Prix trends although certainly the cars are infinitely safer than the ones I raced. And indeed I share your feelings about the number of my friends who were killed, although one must remember they were doing what they most enjoyed in their lives."*

> Louis Stanley wrote in *Behind the Scenes* in 1985, *"The Grand Prix world is a very small one. If a driver dies it means the loss of a friend. When Wolfgang von Trips was killed at Monza the instinctive reflex was to quit a sport that could bring such senseless loss of life, yet such is the gentleness of time that the scars heal".*

Duncan Hamilton

Looking at it from the driver's point of view in 1960, Duncan Hamilton wrote about the dangers in motor racing in his book *Touch Wood*:

> *"We were simply sportsmen paying our way most of the time to participate in a game we thoroughly enjoyed. Did we have any concept of danger? No I don't suppose we did. Motor racing was really a simple extension of everyday road driving. It wasn't the totally different specialised science it has become today. Accepting that it will hurt if you hit it we sped past ditches and trees and walls and telegraph poles since most of us were accustomed to driving pretty quickly on everyday roads in any case. Also in the late 40s and 50s they considered themselves lucky to have survived the War, and every morning a bonus."*

Setting aside this darker aspect of the sport, and with those words in mind, we can celebrate those earlier days of motor racing and the sheer fun that used to characterise motor racing for drivers and spectators alike.

Sid Watkins

In his book *Beyond the Limit* Professor Sid Watkins tells a story about Innes Ireland's sense of fun. Having hired a car from Hertz while he was in the United States, Innes was offered a lift from Sebring by plane. The problem was, what to do with the car? Now it so happened that Hertz had as their advertising slogan at the time, "Pick it up here, drop it there and we'll take care of it." Taking the slogan at its face value, he drove the car towards the hotel swimming pool, jumping out just before it plunged into the water! He phoned Hertz to explain and they brought a television crew with them when they came to retrieve the car and afterwards used the incident to good effect in their publicity!

Mike Hawthorn

In his autobiography *Grand Prix Carpet-Bagger* John Cooper wrote of Mike Hawthorn that he was *"full of fun, loved practical jokes and gave his all to driving fast cars."* That was true of Hawthorn and it was true of many others who in his day enjoyed the sport of motor racing and entertained the enthusiasts who came to watch them.

John Cooper gave me a signed copy of his book and, over the years I have enjoyed the privilege of being able to correspond with, meet, and come to know, many of the famous people in the world of motor sport.

The author's painting of the days when they overtook out on the circuit and not just during pit stops! Stirling Moss about to overtake Reg Parnell to win the Gold Cup at Oulton Park in 1954.

Getting to know celebrities through their biographies can sometimes be disappointing, as was the case for me when I read Robert McCrum's biography of P.G Wodehouse. It revealed that he was nothing like the carefree characters that he portrayed in his books, and humour seldom seemed to spring from his pen spontaneously. But I have never found coming to know those who have become household names through racing fast cars a disappointment. They have all without exception turned out to be, as Bertie Wooster might have said, "good eggs" and what a joy it has been to make their acquaintance and, in some cases, to form deep and lasting friendships.

Duncan Hamilton at Brooklands

Duncan Hamilton was one of the most entertaining and colourful people within the motor racing fraternity I have ever had the pleasure to meet and, for him, motor racing and fun seemed to have been inseparable. In *Touch Wood* he recalled an incident involving him at Brooklands which could surely only have happened to him.

It was before the war, and Gainsborough Pictures were filming "Ask a Policeman". The film was to begin in the fictional village of Turn Bottom Round, ending on the banked circuit of Brooklands. Will Hay's stunt man was to drive a double-decker bus the wrong way round the circuit while a race was supposed to be in progress. All the cars were duly lined up ready when the bus was set off in the opposite direction and the drivers stood by the cars. Then, at the last minute, Freddie Dixon's mechanic, who was to drive his Riley, asked Duncan Hamilton, a young student from the Aeronautical Engineering College, to keep the car's engine running while he briefly went back to the pits. Before he returned the order was given to start and the resourceful young man, taken completely by surprise, jumped in the car and engaged second gear so that the Riley leapt forward with such violence that his goggles slipped down from his forehead, totally obscuring his vision. Braking and raising his goggles, he was surprised to discover that all the other cars had also stopped. The astonished bus driver later told everybody that Hamilton had missed his speeding bus by only three inches!

Duncan Hamilton had an inexhaustible store of amusing anecdotes with which he regaled my wife and I over a very fine lunch which Angela had prepared for us in their home in Somerset. At the same time, of course, he was a serious and gifted racing driver who, among his many successes, won the Le Mans 24 Hour Race with a works C Type Jaguar in 1953.

He epitomised for me an age when motor racing was fun. He began to race in earnest at Goodwood and Silverstone after the war, but it was at Brooklands that his interest was first kindled.

Goodwood in 1949

I have been fascinated by cars from my earliest childhood and recall being horrified when the teacher of my infants' class told us that Moses ground into powder a golden car that the Israelites had made in the wilderness. I couldn't bring myself to forgive the Almighty – until I discovered that I had misheard her and that the idol in question was a golden calf!

My interest in motor racing was first stimulated by a family fun day out at Goodwood on Easter Monday in 1949. It seems like only yesterday. I was twelve years old and remember travelling to Goodwood wedged between my elder brothers David and John in the rear seat of my father's 1935 Morris Oxford. Having previously read the reports of the famous Donington Park Grands Prix of 1937 and 1938 in old copies of *Motor Sport* in the store room of my father's shop, I was certain that it was going to be an exciting experience, and it fully lived up to my expectations. It seemed that everyone on the road from Bishopstoke in Hampshire to Goodwood in Sussex was bound for the same destination, and there was no shortage of sporting types who weaved in and out of the traffic to gain advantage, to the accompaniment of low growls from my father. A cartoon by Brockbank afterwards conveyed a hilarious impression of their unbridled enthusiasm. It showed the drivers of small Morgans and large Bentleys zig zagging from side to side across the road with great relish while avoiding straw bales that were falling from the back of a lorry! The improvised car parks at Goodwood, set in acres of grassland, offered a fascinating array of interesting pre-war cars included Bugattis, Bentleys, and Aston Martins. There was a stately Daimler, whose occupants were enjoying champagne and caviar while sitting around a large hamper laid out upon the grass.

The racing cars could already be heard out on the circuit beyond and so I was anxious to finish our own modest picnic in order to gain my first glimpse of them.

The Duke of Richmond

Years later, in 1986, the 9th Duke of Richmond, who as Freddie March had won the Brooklands Double 12 in 1930, wrote to me about the inadequacies of the arrangements at that time.

> "So you were at that memorable Easter Monday Meeting in 1949. We had nowhere near finished our crowd preparations and if you remember had terrible crowd control problems! However the Goodwood Motor race story is a happy one and I am certain it was the right decision to stop when we did. Woodcote corner and the proximity of the main road cross-road just the other side of the hedge was a very probable battle ground and there was nothing we could do about it! I see you follow motor racing still. I'm afraid I don't, mostly because of considerable old age but partly because to me so much of the spectacle seems to have been lost now all the cars look so much alike. And the drivers resembling spacemen are, of course, more or less invisible anyway! We do still provide test arrangements on occasion, and I'm bound to admit that their velocity today is mind and eye boggling!"

Goodwood Reopened

Fortunately the Earl of March was eventually able to have the circuit made safe and to persuade the authorities to allow Goodwood to be reopened for racing in 1999. He very generously sent three tickets for myself, Kath and our son Michael, so that we could be there to watch the reopening ceremony when he drove around the circuit in the Bristol 400 sports saloon with which his grandfather had opened the circuit originally in 1948. As Lord March came down the finishing straight a Spitfire coming from the opposite direction flew over him, missing the Bristol's roof only by inches. It was most spectacular!

Memories of 1949

My Goodwood Motor Race Meeting programme from 1949.

Back in 1949 there were notices everywhere warning the public that "motor racing is dangerous" but many took no notice of them and found the most precarious vantage points on the top of roofs, in trees and even on the wrong side of the chestnut fencing that lined the outside of the circuit! By standing in one place in comparative safety we found ourselves gradually inching towards the front as others moved away until we could actually hold on to the chestnut fencing to gain a clear view of the cars. The 500cc race was, as always, most entertaining and Stirling Moss, who had been the winner at the first meeting the previous year, was identified as the one to watch. Most impressive of all was the flame-red 4CLT Maserati of Reg Parnell which looked very powerful and modern against an array of elderly E.R.A.s. To my father's delight there were bookmakers at Goodwood that day and he laid a modest amount on each race.

I was mystified by the fact that Reg Parnell's 4CLT Maserati had been entered by Scuderia Ambrosiana and it was many years before I discovered what this actually meant. In 1937 Count Johnny Lurani formed the Scuderia Ambrosiana with Luigi Villoresi and Franco Cortese and named it after St Ambrose, the Patron Saint of Milan. As a member of the team Lurani won a number of races with his 4CM Maserati before the war, and Parnell's Maserati was entered for Goodwood under his name. Years later I sent Count Lurani a painting of him in his 4CM car.

The Bishopstoke Grands Prix

Inspired by that Goodwood experience, the fun of motor racing was celebrated by three young teenagers in the rear garden of number 43 Fair Oak Road, Bishopstoke, long before the days of Scalextric and modern computer games.

David and I persuaded our friend Keith Eaton, who lived a few doors from us, to stage race meetings with our Dinky Toys. They say that the difference between men and boys is the price they pay for their toys, and our cars were inexpensive! I remember buying three 158 Alfa Romeos from the local shop for a total of seven shillings and six pence or 37.5 new pence. We each fielded a team of three cars painted in team colours. I chose British Racing Green, David opted for blue and yellow, these being Prince Bira's colours, while Keith elected to adopt Italian red. Miniature car parks were created with our collections of Dinky Toy road cars. There were improvised garages and pits, and we even lined the course with white strips of paper with Dunlop, Esso and other advertisements painted on them, just like the real thing. The track consisted of a length of cement which bypassed a fish pond and was swept before race meetings. Beyond this the lawn was carefully mown before meetings and

The 23c Dinky Toy Mercedes Benz in Prince Bira's colours.

it was all taken very seriously. Each car was propelled along the course by being released from our hands with some force, after its axles had been well oiled. Bicycle spokes were used to replace worn out axles, and they travelled anything up to forty yards, more often than not keeping all four wheels on the ground throughout. Their positions were recorded and the procedure was repeated for all nine cars according to the number of laps of a Grand Prix in the real world. We shadowed the Formula One calendar so that we could identify a World Champion at the end of the season. It was all so much more fun than the more sophisticated pastimes of youngsters today. With careful use of a file and a hacksaw, a little glue, plasticine, and a lot of imagination, my Alfa Romeos were transformed into B.R.M.s and my 23a "small open racing cars" into an H.W.M.s. Keith's cars became minor works of art but required major reconstruction after each race meeting, while David's 23c Mercedes Benz remained in its standard form. Our eldest brother John naturally regarded the whole enterprise with lofty distain, especially when Keith embarrassed us by explaining to him that one of his cars had a slipping clutch!

Racing in miniature. From left to right: The author, David and Keith.

During the winter months we managed to hold our own "Monte Carlo Rallies" with the use of large quantities of sand, earth, and water, using some of the saloon and sports cars in the Dinky Toy range.

Scalextric

Years later Scalextric arrived and this proved to be great fun while it was also taken fairly seriously. In those days even the racing drivers sometimes competed with each other with slot cars on the eve of a Grand Prix.

In Coventry to launch the Scalextric record bid with Sir John Egan, Air Vice-Marshall Robinson and the Le Mans winning Jaguar.

In 1989, when I was the Vicar of the Parish of All Saints in Bournemouth, I set out to achieve a duration record with a Scalextric Jaguar and a Williams Honda to raise money for the Church Urban Fund. A large layout was built in the Church annexe by Jack Freeman the Church Treasurer and, with the help of Simon Kohler, the Marketing Manager of Hornby Hobbies who provided the cars, I.B.M. who devised the means of recording their progress day and night, the Chase Manhattan Bank, now known as J. P. Morgan, who produced competition forms for the entire nation, and a large number of the church members, our entry was eventually recorded in *The Guinness Book of Records*. The Scalextric Jaguar XJ8, a replica of the car in which Johnny Dumfries won the Le Mans 24 Hours Race, ran non stop for over five weeks on our Church annexe special track. It covered 1771.2 real miles to raise money for the cause! The model car was taken to up London to appear with Roy Castle in the popular television programme "Record Breakers," and it's a record that still stands. The following year we also broke the endurance record for model trains with a Hornby "Lady Patricia" and six coaches.

The record-breaking Scalextric Jaguar alongside "Lady Patricia".

THE HEROIC YEARS

MOTOR RACING is almost as old as the motor car itself, and the main purpose of the earliest races on the Continent of Europe was to demonstrate that these strange, new-fangled horseless carriages, were a viable alternative to the quadrupeds they would replace. Gottlieb Daimler, Wilhelm Maybach and Karl Benz were responsible for inventing the first internal combustion engine which they fitted in the front of a simple chassis with wheels shod with rubber solid tyres at each corner, two seats, a fuel tank, and grossly inadequate brakes. The French were the first to organise motor races which took place on public roads to the amazement, excite-ment and consternation of unsuspecting pedestrians who were sometimes too slow to get out of their way. These primitive cars must have caused a sensation and when they managed not to end up in a ditch, up a tree, against a telegraph pole, or into the spectators, they achieved their object in a great cloud of dust.

The 1894 Trial

The Daimler licence was bought in France by Emile Levassor and Rene Panhard who also sold their engines to Armand Peugeot. Richard Hough and Michael Frostick record in *A History of the World's Racing Cars*, that the very first recorded motoring trial took place in 1894, sponsored by *Le Petit Journal* of Paris. It was regarded as a trial of reliability rather than a race, the award being given to the car which was "without danger, easily handled and of low running cost". An initial entry of over one hundred cars was reduced to nineteen and they set off on 22 July from Paris to Rouen. The first prize of 5000 francs was awarded to Messrs Panhard and Levassor and Les Fils de Peugeot Freres, each of their cars being powered by Daimler engines. Nine cars finished, including a steam driven De Dion driven by the Comte de Dion which was in fact the first to arrive.

Paris-Bordeaux

In 1895, an event was organised by the Automobile Club de France from Paris to Bordeaux and back again, a distance of over more than seven hundred miles. It was sponsored by two wealthy Americans, James Gordon Bennett and William K. Vanderbilt and the prize money amounted to £2,800. Twenty-two cars competed for it and Emile Levassor won the race at an average speed of fifteen mph in a two cylinder 1,200 cc Panhard Levassor. It took him just over two days with the help of a relief driver. In the years that followed, cars with engines of up to sixteen litres joined these competitions but the ineffectiveness of their brakes must have been even more concerning. The first fatal accident occurred in 1898 when the Marquise de Montignac and his mechanic crashed into a tree-lined ditch after colliding with a Benz driven by the Marquis de Montariol. Montariol had taken his hand from the tiller to wave to Montignac and hence the accident! It was during the Paris–Amsterdam–Paris race which was run over 889 miles. The entry had been divided into standard touring cars, of which there were thirty, and forty-three racing cars. These were the heroic years of motor racing when many of the vehicles were equipped with tillers instead of steering wheels and the narrow tyres of their cars were constantly plunging into unforgiving potholes or jumping over stones, shaking the occupants to pieces.

No one has captured the drama and excitement of the earliest years of motor racing better than Gordon Crosby whose sketches appeared in the *Autocar* magazine over many years. His paintings of the first French Grand Prix and the Gordon Bennett Races, seen in conjunction with the rare archive footage of Shell's *The History of Motor Racing*, enable one to gain an impression of what motor racing must have been like in those early days.

The Gordon Bennett Races

In 1900 James Gordon Bennett, the proprietor of the *New York Herald*, sponsored the Paris to Lyons race which was organised by the Automobile Club de Paris with the object of improving the design of the motor car. Enthusiasts have argued ever since that motor racing improves the breed. It was the first of the Gordon Bennett Races and they were held each year until 1905. The cars, all their component parts including their tyres and the drivers, had to be from the same country as the entrant. Trials were held before the races to select the teams, and each country was allowed to enter three cars. All the cars were paced through the towns along the route by bicycles!

In 1901 the race was won by Fernand Charron in a Panhard and in 1902 an Englishman, Selwyn Francis Edge in a 50hp Napier brought the trophy to Great Britain. Benz produced a 90hp Mercedes for the 1903 race which had to be held in Ballyshannon because it was forbidden to close any public roads on the mainland of Britain, and it consisted of seven laps of a closed circuit which added up to 327 miles. Prior to the event a fire destroyed the Benz entries and, in their place, a stripped down 60hp Mercedes won at an average speed of 42.9 mph. The last Gordon Bennett Cup race was won by Leon Thery with his mechanic Muller in a Brasier.

People wondered at the sight of these cars and an enthusiastic observer said that to compare a steam locomotive to a car would be like comparing a gambolling elephant to the flight of a swallow!

Marcel Renault in his 30bhp Renault in the Paris-Madrid race in 1903.

In 1903 the Paris–Madrid race was stopped at Bordeaux after a series of accidents. Marcel Renault was one of those was killed when his car overturned at Coune-Verac, and after this all the races were sensibly confined to roads that were closed and properly policed for the events. The cars that competed in these early races were monsters that stirred up great clouds of dust and dirt from the roads, frequently obscuring them from view. According to William Boddy and Brian Laban's *The history of Motor Racing* the sound of the 9.8 litre 45hp De Dietrich was like that of Gatling machine guns!

The First Grand Prix in Europe

The first French Grand Prix was held near Le Mans in 1906. The makes of car were given numbers and the individual cars were identified with the addition of the letters A, B or C after their number. The winning Renault, driven by Szisz and painted red was timed at 92.2 mph over a flying kilometre. The Renault was equipped with detachable wheel rims and this contributed to its success as it took only two minutes to change a tyre instead of up to fifteen. The race was run in two

David Bruce-Brown with riding mechanic in a Fiat S74, during the French Grand Prix of 1912.

Christian Lautenschlager winning the French Grand Prix in 1914, in his 4.5 litre Mercedes. Followed by the Peugeot of Jules Goux.

stages, each of 385 miles. A Fiat won the race in 1907 and a Mercedes Benz in 1908. After this the race discontinued until 1912.

In 1912 and 1913 the race was won by George Boillot in a Peugeot but in 1914, on the eve of the First World War, the French Grand Prix, which took place near Lyons over a twenty-three mile circuit, was rather ominously won by the Mercedes Benz team which took the first three places led by Christian Lautenschlager.

The first German Grand Prix was held in 1907 in the Taunus Mountains, and the first Italian Grand Prix in 1922 at Monza. The first Belgian Grand Prix took place at Spa in Belgium in 1925, and the first race in the streets of Monaco was in 1929.

The Targa Florio

Cavalieri Florio organised the first Targa Florio in 1906 in the wild Madonie Mountains of Sicily. It then consisted of three laps of a ninety-two mile circuit over difficult roads starting at sea level and rising to a height of 3000 feet. Ten cars took part and it was won by Cagnot's Itala.

In 1907 limits were stipulated on the engine size and weight of the cars. Forty-six cars were set off in intervals and the race was won by Felice Nazzaro at an average speed of 33.5 mph in a Fiat. There were sixteen retirements.

The works Mercedes Benz cars were painted dark red in 1924 so as to ensure a passage untroubled by the fiercely patriotic locals who threw boulders down upon vehicles painted any other colour.

Count Giulio Massetti winning the Targa Florio in his 1914 Grand Prix Mercedes in 1922.

A 'works' Mercedes in Italian red! Winner of the 1924 Targa Florio driven by Christian Werner. 1/18 scale model by CMC.

Alfa Romeos won the Targa Florio seven times between 1923 and 1935 and again in 1950 and 1971. Tazio Nuvolari drove the winning Alfa Romeos in 1931 and 1932.

Rene Dreyfus described his impressions of the Targa Florio in his book *My Two Lives*, a signed copy of which he sent to me. He recalled that the mountain roads were as poor there as they had been in the Paris–Madrid race. Louis Chiron persuaded him to enter the race in 1928 driving his Bugatti Type 37A with his mechanic Jacobs, but they had not been warned to refrain from consuming too much liquid during the days before the race. Consequently Dreyfus and Jacobs were in great discomfort by the third of the five laps and, not wishing to lose time by stopping, they decided to "let it go," only to discover a different form of discomfort! They finished in eighth place!

One competitor, a "diminutive lady," called Elizabeth Junek, drove her Bugatti round the course day after day for a month before the event until she knew it better than anyone. She managed to keep up with the leaders until mechanical problems caused her to drop back to fifth place.

In the 1937 Targa Florio Rene Dreyfus drove a Delahaye 135 with Pietro Ghersi. On the mountain road from Rome to Forli he hit a patch of deep mud which covered his visor and blinded him so that he hit something which turned the car over. Both were thrown out and Pietro sat on the road and kept repeating, "You tell them you were driving," because he had acquired a reputation for turning cars over!

Stirling Moss and Peter Collins won the race in their 300SLR Mercedes Benz in 1955, in spite of leaving the road at one stage and plunging twelve feet down a rocky slope.

The Mille Miglia

In 1927 the Mille Miglia was held for the first time over 1000 miles of Italian roads. Enzo Ferrari, who drove in some of the earlier races, wrote *"the Mille Miglia not only provided enormous technical advances during its three decades, it really did breed champions."*

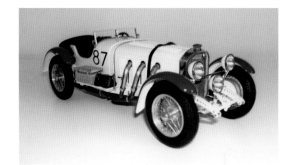

The SSKL Mercedes with which Rudolf Caracciola won the 1931 Mille Miglia. Model by CMC.

Tazio Nuvolari

In *Winners* edited by Brian Laban, Mike Kettleworth describes how Tazio Nuvolari won the Mille Miglia in 1930 driving a 1759 cc Alfa Romeo. *"Nuvolari won the Mille Miglia in classic style. Varzi appeared set for victory as he neared the end of the marathon drive, but he had a huge surprise in store. Nuvolari had driven like a demon to close the gap and, espying what were obviously the lights of Varzi's car ahead in the early morning gloom, he switched his own lights off and crept up behind. With less than two miles to go, Nuvolari stole ahead of his rival."* In 1933 Varzi's honour was satisfied when, driving a T51Bugatti, he had a race long duel with Nuvolari's 8C Alfa Romeo in the Monaco Grand Prix, the two exchanging the lead for lap after lap over the entire race, bringing the crowds to their feet. That time it was Varzi who crossed the finishing line in first place.

The great Nuvolari was a legend in his own lifetime and an endless source of anecdotes. In 1925 he had a trial in a P2 Alfa Romeo at Monza but when the car's gearbox seized on a corner he crashed into a tree breaking both his legs. At that period in his life he was racing motorcycles and he was ordered by the hospital doctors not to race again for a month. The following week, with both legs in plaster, mechanics had to stand each side of him to prop him up on his machine for the start of a race – which he won!

Piero Taruffi

Piero Taruffi drove a 2.3 litre Bugatti in the 1930 Mille Miglia and finished in fortieth place. He drove fourteen Mille Miglia's in all and won at his last attempt in 1957, driving a 4-litre works Ferrari. He displayed in his study a painting I sent of him winning the Swiss Grand Prix in 1952 in a Ferrari and wrote, *"If you ever come to Rome please come and see it."*

Rene Dreyfus

Dreyfus drove a Delahaye in the 1938 Mille Miglia with his mechanic Maurice Varet. They were second when they reached Rome but then a rock pierced the car's radiator and he had to stop frequently for water. Nevertheless he finished in fourth place, only two minutes after the third-placed car.

The 300SLR Mercedes with which Stirling Moss won the 1955 Mille Miglia. 1/18 scale model by CMC.

Stirling Moss

Stirling Moss won the event in 1955 with Dennis Jenkinson in a works 300SLR Mercedes Benz and not surprisingly regarded it as the greatest test of his career. One has nothing but admiration for those who competed in, let alone won, what lesser mortals would consider to be a truly a terrifying event. The Mille Miglia was banned in 1957 when the Marques de Portago crashed into the crowd, causing his death and that of a number of spectators.

Racing in the United States

Motor racing got off to an early start in the United States of America with races for the Vanderbilt Cup from 1905 and the 500 mile race in Indianapolis from 1911. European cars entered the
American races from the earliest days and, at the same time, the Duesenbergs made a good
account of themselves in European events. The purpose of the Indianapolis 500 has always been
to provide exciting entertainment for the spectators rather than to develop and improve the motor
car. It succeeded in that purpose as the oval banked circuit, paved with bricks, drew a crowd of
300,000. There were 41 starters in 1911 and the race was won by a locally-produced Marmon with
a Fiat and a Mercedes finishing third and fourth. When the Formula One World Drivers' Championship was introduced in 1950 points were awarded for the Indianapolis 500 Race and added
to the total.

Brooklands

In Britain the law requiring every car to be preceded by a man carrying a red flag was repealed in
1896 and the London and Brighton run was inaugurated to celebrate it. However a new law was
introduced prohibiting any car from being driven on the public roads in this country in excess of
twenty miles per hour.

It was to meet this situation that the Brooklands circuit was built on the estate of Hugh
Fortescue Locke-King in 1906. He saw that it was necessary for the development of fast British
cars that they should be tested at sustained high speeds in this country, and he received the instant
support for his venture of Lord Northcliffe and Lord Montague of Beaulieu.

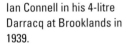

Ian Connell in his 4-litre
Darracq at Brooklands in
1939.

Brooklands was officially opened on June 28 in 1907 when Selwyn Edge established a twenty-
four hour distance record by driving around the circuit for 1581 miles at an average speed of
65.905 mph in his British Napier. The first race on the 2.75 miles of track, for the Marcel Renault
Memorial Plate was won by H.C. Tryon in another Napier.

Some complained that Brooklands lacked the appeal of the European road races because the
cars looked comparatively distant and were dwarfed by the width of the track and the distance of
the spectators from it. But, in spite of this Brooklands soon drew the fastest and most powerful
racing cars from overseas to this country, and it encouraged the development of competitive cars
at home. The races were organised by the British Automobile Racing Club whose motto was "the
right crowd and no crowding". But motor racing at Brooklands was not the exclusive preserve of
the wealthy, and its popularity with the nation as a whole was firmly established by the time that
the Second World War forced its closure. It drew characters like Parry Thomas with his aero-

engined monster called "Babs," Henry "Tim" Birkin in his streamlined single seater "Blower" Bentley, George Eyston, Freddie Richmond and Johnny Lurani in their M.G.s, Raymond Mays, Prince Bira and others in their E.R.A.s and Dick Seaman in his Delage. The list of course is endless. The faster the cars were driven the higher they climbed up the banking, sometimes, sadly to their destruction.

Tim Birkin in his 4.5 litre "Blower" Bentley in the British Empire Trophy race at Brooklands, in 1932.

Parry Thomas survived Brooklands only to lose his life in "Babs" when racing at speed on the Pendine Sands in West Wales. His car was buried deep in the sand out of respect for its owner and remained there for many years but is now in a museum near the site of the tragic accident.

In the preface to his magnificent work *The History of Brooklands* William Boddy, the unrivalled authority on the subject, wrote that *"many of the world's great drivers competed frequently at Brooklands and indeed, men such as John Cobb, Whitney Straight, Woolf Barnato, Sammy Davis, Kaye Don, Sir Henry Birkin, Bt., Sir Henry Seagrave and many others gained their early experience at the Track, while Parry Thomas was Brooklands. They paid less heed to fame and drove there because, like Water Rat with boats, they enjoyed 'messing about in cars'."*

Donington Park

Donington Park had been sold to John Gillies Shields by Lord Donington and it became a prisoner-of-war camp for German soldiers during the First World War. Two of the prisoners managed to tunnel their way out but were later recaptured. Two others climbed over the barbed wire fence and one successfully made his way back to Germany by means of a ship from Tilbury.

Some years later Fred Cranmer, who raced a team of motorcycles, persuaded the Shields to construct a racing circuit on the estate for motorcycle races and on March 25th 1933 and the circuit, which measured 2 miles 327 yards was widened and resurfaced at a cost of £12,000 before the first motor race took place. M.Gs and Austins took part and the race was won at an average speed of 56 mph. For 1935 the circuit was enlarged to 2 miles 971 yards and the first Donington Grand Prix took place. It was over 125 laps or 318 miles and most notable amongst the entrants were Guiseppi Farina's Maserati, Raymond Sommer's Alfa Romeo, Prince Bira's and Earl Howe's

B. C. APPS '97

Hermann Lang's W125 Mercedes having lapped Raymond Mays' E.R.A. at Donington Park in 1937.

E.R.A.s, Freddie Dixon's Riley and Richard Shuttleworth's Alfa Romeo. The narrow track weaved through unspoilt countryside and was lined by trees in places. Spectators were able to sit at the side of the circuit and they drew their legs back as the cars passed!

Farina started from pole position but retired, and the race was won by Shuttleworth from Earl Howe. In 1936 Dick Seaman won the Donington Grand Prix in an Alfa Romeo which he shared with Hans Reuch. Both the Mercedes Benz and Auto Union teams then wanted to gain his services and, after choosing to drive for Mercedes, Seaman was largely responsible for bringing the two German teams to Donington the following year.

When in 1937 and 1938 the mighty Mercedes Benz and Auto Union teams came over to take part in the Donington Grands Prix the British crowd wondered at the sound and fury of the German cars and, not least, at the spectacle of them taking to the air at Melbourne Rise.

The 1937 Grand Prix was won by Rosemeyer's Auto Union followed by the two Mercedes Benz of von Brauchitsch and Caracciola, and in 1938 the finishing order was Nuvolari's Auto Union followed the Mercedes of Lang and Seaman. The British cars were outclassed but many years later Ian Connell, who drove his E.R.A. told me that the E.R.A.s won the team prize as both the German teams suffered retirements while the British team remained intact. He also commented that he was in the most perfect position to watch the race as the German cars lapped him!

The drama of those two events is recalled by Christopher Hilton in his book *Hitler's Grands Prix in England* and he describes how, after coming to England in 1938, the threat of war almost caused the two German teams to be withdrawn back to Stuttgart before the race. The Germans were relieved to discover that the good manners of the British towards their visitors prevented any unpleasantness while they remained in this country.

THE "BENTLEY BOYS"

T IM BIRKIN served as a fighter pilot in the First World War and he discovered afterwards that civilian life offered none of the excitement to which he had become accustomed. He complained that each day became *"more vapid and tepid than the last"* - until he found an opportunity to enjoy life and to escape its boredom by racing Bentleys!

W.O.Bentley

Walter Owen Bentley, who designed the Bentleys, had been largely responsible for designing the engine of the Sopwith Camel aircraft which had become famous in combat during the Great War. His cars were fast, well engineered, and represented the most modern technology of his day. Like the Continental manufacturers, W.O. realised that the surest way to find customers was to demonstrate the outstanding qualities of his cars on the race track.

In due course W.O. built the 3-litre and 4.5-litre models, the Speed Sixes and, thanks to Tim Birkin, the "Blower" cars. He chose the Le Mans 24 Hours Race as the principal means of advertising their worth to the world.

Bentleys also excelled at Brooklands, and in 1929 W.O. Bentley decided to sit in the passenger seat of Tim Birkin's car as his riding mechanic for the Brooklands 500.

He explained later why he had done this. *"I thought the mechanics were beginning to consider themselves heroes"*, he said, adding, *"After the race I realised they were right!"*

4½-litre "Blower" Bentley. 1/18 scale model by Minichamps.

Le Mans

I drove around the ten miles of the famous Le Mans circuit in my Ford Sierra many years after I had listened with wrapt attention in the 1950s to the brief reports of the race which were offered on the radio by the B.B.C. and, in bed at night, carried in my mind an impression of the Jaguars and Aston Martins fighting the Ferraris for position in the darkness. Much later Tony Brooks described to me how wretched the experience could be when blinding rain filled the open cockpit of his car with water and soaked him to the skin! Perhaps that was why I always chose to drive an Aston Martin DB2 in my dreams!

Les Vingt-quatre Heures du Mans was the brainchild of two Frenchmen, Charles Faroux and George Durand, who obtained 100,000 francs from Emile Coquille to stage the first event in 1923. Later Coquille also gave the Rudge Whitworth Cup. One British car entered that initial race and it was a 3-litre Bentley driven by John Duff and Clement. They finished a very creditable fourth and would have finished higher up had their car not been slowed by a leaky fuel tank. It established the fastest lap at 66.70 mph.

W.O. Bentley was at first opposed to competing at Le Mans in 1923 as he thought that his Bentley would not survive the demands of a twenty-four hour race. But he decided at the very last minute to travel to Le Mans to watch his car and was captivated by the drama of the event. The twenty-four race was a test of the cars' lighting systems as much as mechanical parts. One unusual feature of these early races was that all the cars had to drive for the first twenty laps with their hoods erected.

A "Blower" Bentley at Le Mans in 1930 driven by Benjafield and Ramponi. It retired after 20 hours.

The "Heavy Lorries."

The Bentleys were described by Ettoire Bugatti as "heavy lorries" as they weighed nearly two tons and were twelve feet long, but they were also impressively fast.

After 1923 the Grand Prix d'Endurance became an annual event for Bentleys and they were so successful that they threatened to make the race their own.

Their drivers became known as the "Bentley Boys" and they have been described as being flamboyant millionaires who, when not partying, were winning races! Woolf Barnato's parties went on from ten in the evening until six the following morning and they were said to have cost him from £10,000 to £15,000! There was John Duff and Dr Dudley Benjafield, a Harley Street physician, who was otherwise known as "Benjy", Sammy Davis who wrote for the *Autocar* magazine and who once described how the wind *"howled like a host of demons"* as he drove his Bentley at top speed, Glen Kidston who was quite fearless, having served in submarines during the First War as a Lieutenant Commander and Tim Birkin, a member of a Nottinghamshire lace-making family.

The "Blower" Bentleys

Birkin was responsible for developing the supercharged Bentleys, an idea that was originally opposed by W.O. who firmly believed that there was "no substitute for cubic inches." However Birkin had the financial support of the Hon. Dorothy Paget, who was a racehorse owner, and the technical expertise of Amherst Villiers. The supercharged Bentleys were prepared on Dorothy Paget's premises at Welwyn and they developed 240bhp compared with the

130bhp power of the unsupercharged 4.5-litre car. Fifty-four "Blower" Bentleys were produced for private owners and Birkin himself became legendary at Brooklands with his single seater version. The "Blower" cars performed best at sustained high speeds and were therefore more suited to Brooklands than Le Mans. Birkin was once challenged to race the Blue Train from the South of France to Calais in his uniquely rakish Bentley sports saloon by Gurney Nutting and he won the wager.

Bentleys at Le Mans

Duff and Clement returned to the fray in 1924 as the only British entry and beat all comers at an overall average speed of 53.78 mph. This was not what the French had come to see, and it was achieved in spite of the fact that much vital time was lost in the course of the race when a prolonged search had to be made to find the car's keys within the recesses of its bodywork!

The following year two Bentleys, driven again by Duff/Clement and Kensington-Moir/Benjafield, were at Le Mans, but the first retired after a fire engulfed its engine and the second when it ran out of fuel too soon for it to be allowed by the rules to take on any more.

Three Bentleys came to the Sarthe circuit in 1926 but one driven by Davis/Benjafield retired in the twenty-third hour when it crashed on the Mulsanne Corner. A second, driven by Duller and Clement, retired with a valve failure, and a third, driven by Thistlethwayte and Gallop, suffered a similar fate.

The Bentley of Frank Clement and Leslie Callingham leading the Le Mans race in 1927.

The Crash at White House Corner

In 1927 the Bentleys carried the racing numbers 1, 2 and 3, and No 3, driven by Benjafield/Davis, won the event at an average speed of 61.32 mph. The car driven by Clement and Callingham and the 4.5-litre car driven by d'Erlanger and Duller were both eliminated in a multiple crash at White House on the thirty-fifth lap. No 3 had also been involved in the collision and sustained a buckled front wheel in addition to other damage at the front. Its two drivers had to rely upon a policeman's torch strapped to their windscreen pillar to compensate for the loss of a headlamp, but still managed to win the race after a most heroic effort to haul in the leading car.

In *The Art of Gordon Crosby*, Peter Garnier described the multiple accident. The Bentley of Callingham, while leading the race and a lap ahead of the other two Bentleys, arrived at White House to find a Schneider blocking the road. *"Callington took to the ditch rather than hit the Schneider, and was thrown out of the car on to the road. Next came Thelusson's Fasto, which under violent braking snaked through the gap – to stop, facing the wrong way, on the left side of the road. Then came the two 3-litre Bentleys – first George Duller's car, which joined Callington's in the ditch, knocking the former back on to the road. Thus, No 1 the 4.5 litre and No 2 a 3-litre were out of the race. Sammy Davis, in the second 3-litre had some sort of advance warning of the situation, seeing dust, head-lamps pointing in odd directions, and stones and dirt on the road. He was thus able to get some speed off the car, and cannoned through the gap, bouncing from Schneider to Bentley to Fasto – and drove on to the pits. Though the car was badly damaged, and handled abominably, Sammy Davis and Dr Benjafield went on to win the race"*

The winning car was brought to the Savoy Hotel, still caked with the mud and grime of the race, where the team stood around to toast it. The extravagant post-race celebrations of the Bentley Boys were legendary as they worked hard and played hard and were transported by their craving for speed.

In 1928 the three Bentleys were joined by a team of two Aston Martins, both of which were to retire. The Woolf Barnato and Bernard Rubin Bentley won the race, in spite of finishing with a radiator that was bone dry, at a speed of 69.11 mph. The Tim Birkin Chassagne car finished fifth after establishing a new lap record at 79.29 mph, and a third car driven by Clement and Benjafield retired after running in third place.

Their Greatest Victory

W.O. Bentley's greatest victory came in 1929 when he entered no less than five cars for Le Mans. Barnato/Tim Birkin won the race at a speed of 73.63 mph. Dunfee/Kidson finished in second place, Benjafield/d'Erlanger came third while the car that was driven by Clement/Chassagne was fourth. The fifth car, driven by Rubin/Earl Howe retired on the seventh lap with magneto problems.

The Last Works Entry

1930 was the last year that W.O. Bentley entered his cars for Le Mans. The Speed Six of Barnato/Kidston won the race at a speed of 78.88 mph. A second car driven by Clement/Watney finished second, while a third, driven by Sammy Davis/Dunfee crashed and retired on lap 21. Two super-

The Benjafield/d'Erlanger Bentley at Le Mans in 1929.

charged "Birkin Blower" Bentleys were entered privately by Dorothy Paget but, although they were driven by four of the Bentley Boys, both retired in the course of the race.

The Bentley Boys were modest before the microphones and cameras after their victories and seemed to be embarrassed by all the attention. One of them said, *"We are both very happy to have won this wonderful race and think you are all very nice to have made such a fuss of us."* His team mate added, *"Yes, I quite agree. All I'm waiting for now is a drink!"*

Victims of the Depression

Bentleys became victims of the Wall Street Crash as the Depression that followed brought them into financial difficulty. It has been said that a whole terrace of houses could have been bought for the price of a Bentley and previously wealthy customers were no longer able to afford these cars. Consequentally the firm was taken over by Rolls Royce.

In 1931 a privately entered Bentley retired on the first lap and the race was won by an Alfa Romeo driven by Sommer and Chinetti. The next year another privately entered car retired and the race was won by Sommer/Nuvolari again in an Alfa Romeo. It was left to Aston Martin to continue to carry the flag at Le Mans and eventually success came to them in 1959 under the ownership of David Brown.

When I asked Manfred von Brauchitsch in 1994 which in his opinion was the best of all the British cars he replied without hesitation "the Bentley." He must have had in mind the "heavy lorries" that took on the 7.1-litre supercharged SSK Mercedes Benz of Rudolf Caracciola. W.O. Bentley's cars had certainly left their mark on the world and neither they, nor the Bentley Boys who drove them, will ever be forgotten.

The Newsome/Peacock Aston Martin at Le Mans in 1931.

RAYMOND MAYS
AND THE E.R.A.

RAYMOND MAYS was an enthusiastic champion of motor racing and, in his foreword to *British Motor Cars 1950–1951* compiled by A.H. Lukins, he listed many of the important ways in which motor racing had impacted upon ordinary family saloons. He wrote:

> *"Four–wheel braking systems were regular racing 'wear' before the tourers and saloons of the early twenties started sprouting those little red triangles astern. The late J.G. Parry Thomas, whose fatal crash at Pendine Sands in 1927 terminated the career of perhaps the greatest designer–constructor–driver of all time, developed torsion bar springs on his racing car at a date when not one motorist in a hundred had even heard of the device. Hemispherical cylinder heads, which find a place on the cream of Europe's high-performance production cars in 1950, were featured before the first World War in the Grand Prix designs of Peugeot and others. Then consider independent rear suspension by means of swinging half axles, currently employed on hundreds of thousands of small family cars in Central Europe and Germany; it was as far back as 1923, if my memory isn't at fault, that a German racing car called the Rumpler pioneered the swing-axle layout."*

His Early Motoring Career

Raymond Mays enjoyed driving fast cars and he devoted his life to creating, developing and racing them. He became best known in later years for being the "father" of the B.R.M., but before the war gained great distinction both as a racing driver and as the one who was principally responsible for producing the E.R.A. racing cars. He was enthusiastic about speed from a very early age and was encouraged by his father who entered his own Napiers and Vauxhalls in local hillclimbs and speed trials. Raymond first met Amherst Villiers, who was to become important to his motor racing career, when they were both at Oundle School. After being commissioned in the Grenadier Guards during the First World War and serving in France, he and Villiers met up again at Cambridge where Ray, as he was known, was given a Speed Model Hillman by his father. The two friends tuned and modified the car and at the Inter-Varsity Hillclimb at Aston Clinton surprised those who push started it, as it catapulted away from them! He made the best time of the day. Then he managed to acquire some discarded engine parts of a works Hillman from two of the directors at the Hillman works in Coventry and, after he and Villiers had fitted them to his own car, he competed successfully in two handicap races at Brooklands.

The Brecia Bugattis

Next he purchased a Brecia Bugatti and eventually added a second. Calling them "Cordon Bleu" and "Cordon Rouge," he won all the main hill climb events with them, creating new records in the process. Then he met Peter Berthon who was an R.A.F. cadet at Cranwell near Bourne. He joined Mays and Villiers in their efforts to produce high performance cars and Mays raced a much modified a 2-litre Targa Florio Mercedes which performed so impressively that the works sent an eight-cylinder car over from Germany for him to race at Brooklands. Next came the Vauxhall Villiers, based on a 1922 works Tourist Trophy car and, in 1933, an Invicta. Finally the White Riley was developed from which eventually the E.R.A. was born.

The author's 1936 Riley Adelph.

E.R.A. models by Matchbox. Models of Yesteryear.

The Riley Adelphi

In the 1966, when I was the assistant curate of St Mary's Andover, I bought a 1936 Riley Adelphi from a garage in the Portobello Road for £150. After its body was resprayed and its radiator and headlamps rechromed, it looked very splendid and I was particularly proud of its affinity to the E.R.A. which was easily recognisable beneath its long bonnet.

English Racing Motors

The E.R.A. factory was established in the Old Maltings in the grounds of Eastgate House, Raymond Mays' family home at Bourne in Lincolnshire. Rileys produced new parts for the much modified engine; Peter Berthon and Murray Jamieson were responsible for the supercharger, Reid Railton designed the Chassis, and the cars' distinctive single-seater bodies were built by Thompson and Taylor at Brooklands. Humphrey Cook backed the enterprise financially and the 1.5-litre supercharged racing cars were built to compete at home and on the Continent in races for Voiturette, as opposed to Grand Prix, cars. The works team of three cars, led by Raymond Mays with Ken Richardson as chief mechanic and test driver, and Peter Berthon as Team Manager, was augmented by a number of privately-owned models driven by Prince Bira, Dick Seaman, Ian Connell, Arthur Dobson, the Band leader Billy Cotton and many others. The cars won no less than fourteen races in 1937 and Raymond Mays himself had many successes, including establishing the lap record on the Mountain Course at Brooklands at 84.31mph. He set a new world record of 89.73 for one kilometre from a standing start, beating the previous record of 88.87 mph by John Cobb in his 23 litre Napier Railton.

The works E.R.A.s were finished in pale green but even more striking were the cars of Prince Birabongse which had hyacinth blue bodies and primrose yellow chassis and wheels. They became the recognised racing colours of Siam.

Prince Bira

Prince Bira was the nephew of the King who was the subject of "The King and I". He was educated in England and went to Eton and Cambridge. He was passionate about motor racing from early childhood and in 1935 his cousin, Prince Chula, bought him an E.R.A. for his twenty-first birthday. Eventually he had no less than three of the cars from Bourne, each of which was given a name. He would visit them in their garages at night, as though they possessed intelligent minds, and he wrote in his book *Bits and Pieces* that in the course of a 200 mile race in the Isle of Man, he patted the cockpit side of "Romulus," or R2B, and told the car that it had now taken the lead!

His other E.R.A.s were "Remus" R5B and "Hanuman" R12B.

With "Romulus" he won the Imperial Trophy and the London Grand Prix at Crystal Palace, and the BRDC Road Race at Brooklands in 1938. He also won the Sydenham Trophy at Crystal Palace in 1939. With "Remus" he won the Albi Grand Prix in 1936, and with "Hanuman" the Campbell Trophy and the Siam Trophy at Brooklands in 1938, and the Nuffield Trophy at Donington in 1939.

Prince Bira with 'Hanuman' in the Campbell Trophy race at Brooklands in 1938.

Bira won the B.R.D.C Gold Star three years running and, writing in the Autocar in August 1939 his cousin Prince Chula disclosed that, in spite of his outstanding successes, the White Mouse Team ran at a loss. The expenses in 1938, including wages, spares and repairs had come to £4,326 while the income, consisting of prize money amounted to £2,933. This was considered to be a satisfactory outcome and Prince Chula's only concern was to refute the charge that, in gaining their success, they had spent more than others.

In 1985 I posted a painting of Prince Bira driving "Hanuman" in the Campbell Trophy at Brooklands to the Palace at Bangkok. Many weeks went by before it was eventually returned with a note saying that he was not in residence. While pondering where I might send it next, I was saddened to read a notice in "The Times" that he had died in a London Hospital after collapsing with a heart attack in the Underground.

E.R.A.s after the War

War brought racing to an end for E.R.A.s, as for everyone else, but the cars were to re-emerge after the war to race again in private hands, while Raymond Mays focused his attention on his ambitious attempt to create a car that would be capable of racing in all the major Grands Prix throughout the world on equal terms.

Humphrey Cook re-registered the E.R.A. Company in Dunstable in 1946 and produced three cars, GP 1, 2 and 3 with which to compete in the new Formula for 1.5-litre supercharged cars, but the demands of the project were too great and it was abandoned. A G-Type Bristol-engined car was raced by Stirling Moss but eventually it was sold to Bristol cars and became the basis for the Bristol 450 Le Mans cars.

Bob Gerard

Bob Gerard drove his own E.R.A.s as did his wife Joan. He was known as "Mr. Bob" to his mechanics and others, and began racing at Brooklands before the war with a Riley.

In 1946 he bought three E.R.A.s, R4A, R14B and R6B and restored them in the workshop of Parr's, his familiy's business in Leicestershire. He was often the fastest of the British drivers and was third in the Ulster Trophy Race in 1946 behind Bira's E.R.A. and Parnell's 4CLT Maserati. He enlarged the engine of R4A to two litres in his own workshop and with it put up the fastest time of the day at Prescott. He finished second to Parnell's Maserati in the first Goodwood Meeting in September 1948 and third in the British Grand Prix at Silverstone behind the Maseratis of Villoresi and Ascari. In 1949 he was second in the British Grand Prix to Baron de Graffenried's Maserati.

In 1986 I sent Bob Gerard a painting of him winning the British Empire Trophy in 1950 and he wrote the following in a Christmas card from himself and Joan.

Bob Gerard's E.R.A. in the British Empire Trophy race in 1950.

I am most appreciative of your excellent paintings. The latter one showing Cuth, myself and Reg Parnell struck a very strong chord in my memory as the positioning of the cars appears odd. It is at Parkfield Corner, the first some one quarter of a mile downhill from the start. Cuth got a flier and led all of us away with so much enthusiasm that he is in fact departing straight on down Bray Hill with all wheels locked, while Reg and I are positioning to turn right round Parkfield as intended. Later in the race it got very slippery there and I did same thing, losing about 30 seconds – luckily by then the lead was adequate to remain in front!

Bob Gerard phoned me the following year and spoke about the time he beat Ken Wharton in the much more powerful V16 B.R.M. at Charterhall in Scotland. Wharton was leading the race but Gerard *"gave him a run for his money and caused him to run wide on the last bend."* He told me that he was having a bungalow built with picture rails just so that he could hang the three paintings I had sent him over the years, as he disliked having nails knocked in the walls!

I wrote to Joan when Bob died but a close friend rang to tell me that she was in a nursing home and unable to reply.

Ian Connell

Ian Connell was one of the British amateur drivers, sometimes referred to as "the chaps", who had the means to drive fast cars at Brooklands and elsewhere in the 1930s just for the fun of it. He did occasionally drive for money, as when he issued the following challenge in *Autocar* magazine in 1939. *"I am willing to challenge Mr. Hunter or any other owner of a fast sports car to, say, five laps of the Campbell circuit for a wager to be decided upon, driving the 4-litre unsupercharged Darracq that I am now running on the road. This car carries full touring equipment, including windscreen, hood and headlights and runs on normal pump fuel."*

Many rose to the challenge but it was settled by Connell's Darracq being taken on by Count Heydon's 3.5-litre Delahaye. The Delahaye won, but Count Heydon had failed to reveal that his car would be driven by the highly talented Arthur Dobson! Ian was compensated for this by being invited by the Count to partner Rob Walker at Le Mans that year driving the Delahaye. The two finished in a very respectable fifth place in a race that was won by the French ace Jean-Pierre Wimille in a Bugatti.

Educated at Marlborough College, Connell studied engineering at Cambridge where he was a contemporary of Richard Seaman. He joined the Cambridge University Automobile Club and raced his M.G. Midget. He also drove a Singer Nine at Le Mans in 1935. After university he and a friend bought a garage which they called Monaco Motors. He once explained to me that the name had been produced from their two names, Peter MONkhouse and Ian COnnell. The business was sold after Peter was killed in the Mille Miglia.

Ian first raced at Brooklands in 1934 and won the BRDC 500 in 1935 in his Vale Special.

He also drove a Monza Alfa Romeo and, with his E.R.A. R6B, came second to Prince Bira in the London Grand Prix of 1937, and eighth in the Donington Park Grand Prix the same year. In 1938 he bought a Lago Talbot and came second in the Fastest Sports Cars Challenge in 1939. He broke his class record in the Lago Talbot at 129.36 mph and, because of the outbreak of war, it stands for all time.

Ian was Commissioned in the Royal Army Service Corps and served in North Africa, Italy and Germany, but then quickly returned to motor racing in the very changed circumstances which prevailed after the war. He bought the ex Bira E.R.A. "Remus" from Tony Rolt and competed in the Grand Prix des Nations at Geneva in 1946. Eventually he sold the E.R.A. and raced a 4CLT Maserati instead. In 1948 he took part in the Tourist Trophy Race in an ex Seaman 2-litre Aston Martin with Dudley Holland and led the twenty-four hour race after twenty-one hours before crashing off the road. In his last race, driving the Aston Marin again with Dudley Holland, he finished in third place. Over a number of years I gave Ian Connell four paintings each of which

Ian Connell's E.R.A. being followed by Bernd Rosemeyer's Auto Union at Donington Park in 1938.

he displayed in his home and was obviously delighted to receive. One was of him at Donington Park in 1938 being overtaken by Bernd Rosemeyer's Auto Union. He wrote:

> "I have it on the wall in my study and it brings back happy memories of those days when one drove for the pleasure and excitement and not for money.
>
> It is funny to think that one entered events such as the Donington Grand Prix with no hope of winning (although we did win the Team Prize as one Mercedes and one Auto Union retired!) but, as you say, we had a good view of the race."

He wrote that my painting of the E.R.A. showed how he used to drive in open neck shirts with sleeves rolled up and no seat belt but he added that he gave up the open neck shirt after being stung by a wasp at Albi! He added that he would be able to bequeath one of my paintings to each of his grand daughters and one to his daughter, all of whom took a keen interest in his past motor racing.

I sent a further painting of him at Shelsley Walsh and this was his reply.

> "I always enjoyed Shelsley Walsh although I do not remember it as a very successful hunting ground – however I did manage the sports car record in 1939 in the Lago Talbot which, due to the intervention of the war, remained in my name for quite a long time!
>
> I am enclosing a photograph of me at Shelsley in case it is of interest to you. I had two E.R.A. R6Bs before the war and R5B after the war. As far as I know they are both still running but I do not know who has them.
>
> In about 1947 I had a short season driving Raymond Sommer's 4CLT Maserati in Grands Prix (rather different to modern G.P.s!)
>
> I occasionally see the wonderful Lago Talbot and it looks exactly the same as when I had it. How nice to have it called a Talbot and not a Darracq! I do not want to part with any of my photographs of it but if you are keen to replace yours I could arrange for a copy to be made.
>
> I hope you will have a happy, and no doubt busy(!) Christmas and that the New Year will bring all you wish for."

One of my paintings was of Ian driving an E.R.A. R6B with twin Arnott superchargers. There are only black and white photographs of the car but he had told me that its body and wheels had been painted navy blue and that the chassis was a silver grey. He explained that the manufacturers of the superchargers had asked him to carry out an experiment by using the twin superchargers on the E.R.A. and so the front of the car had to be modified with an elongated bonnet to accommodate them. It had not been a success as it was too hot for the pistons which melted as a result! *"We reverted to the normal Roots blower."*

With the signed photograph of his E.R.A. at Shelsley Walsh in 1946 Ian sent me a sample of paint that was similar to that in which his Talbot Lago was finished. He was pleased with a further

Ian Connell at Shelsley Walsh in 1946.

painting I gave him of the Talbot Lago speeding on the banking at Brooklands.

He wrote on his Christmas card to me one year, *"Whenever I sit at my desk I see the Talbot Lago (Darraq) bearing down on me and it reminds me that I had promised to sign your E.R.A. book"*. He called one afternoon on my vicarage in Southbourne soon afterwards. We talked of his motor racing exploits of course and he signed my copy of *The History of English Racing Automobiles Limited* by David Weguelin.

I last saw Ian Connell in 2002 at the Memorial Service of Rob Walker in St Luke's Church Sydney Street and the reception at the Royal Chelsea Hospital afterwards.

He passed a way on March 1st the following year at the age of 89.

THE GOLDEN AGE

FRENCH BUGATTIS dominated the Grand Prix scene at the end of the 1920s and William Grover, an Englishman who would be executed during the war for assisting the French Underground, won the first Monaco Grand Prix in 1929 with his 2.3-litre supercharged T35B painted in British Racing Green. Rene Dreyfus won the race in the following year in another T35B, which he and his brother Maurice had bought for $325. In the same event Rudolf Caracciola's more thirsty 7.1-litre supercharged Mercedes SSK sports car was relegated to third place having had to stop for fuel. Yet another Bugatti won the race in 1931 but after this the Italians came back strongly with two Alfa Romeos and a Maserati claiming the first three places in 1932. The next year witnessed a thrilling duel between Varzi's Bugatti and Nuvolari's Alfa Romeo which Varzi eventually won.

The New Formula

Germany grasped its opportunity to return to motor racing in style when a new Formula, limiting the dry weight of the cars to 750 kg, was introduced in 1934. Hitler had agreed to grant 450,000 Reichmarks annually to both Mercedes Benz and Auto Union to ensure that German cars would dominate, but this represented only a fraction of what the two teams actually invested in the sport.

Auto Union had been formed by joining the four companies of Horch, Audi, Wanderer and DKW, and Dr Ferdinand Porsche designed the A-Type Auto Union with a V16 engine of 4.4-litres situated between the driver and the rear wheels, and a streamlined body unlike anything that had been seen before. More conventionally, Mercedes Benz produced the W25 with a straight eight engine of 3.36-litres in the front and a supercharger which screamed in high pitched defiance around the circuits. It too had a streamlined body, the shape of which had been influenced by the special bodied SSK with which von Brauchitsch had won at Avus in 1931.

Silver Arrows by CMC. W125 Mercedes Benz and C-Type Auto Union.

"Silver Arrows"

The German cars became known as "Silver Arrows," after the removal of their white paint and filler had lightened them sufficiently to conform to the rules, and the two teams were responsible for what many call the Golden Age of Motor Racing. Auto Unions won the German, Swiss and Italian Grands Prix in 1934 while Mercedes Benz won in the Eifelrennen, the Coppa Acerbo in Pescara, and the Spanish Grand Prix.

In 1935 the engine of the B-Type Auto Union was enlarged to 4.9-litres and that of the W25 Mercedes Benz to 3.9. Mercedes were dominant that year as the increased power of the Auto Union proved difficult for anyone to control. Nuvolari managed

Hans Stuck's Auto Union leading Rudolf Caracciola's Mercedes in the Italian Grand Prix at Monza in 1935.

Manfred Von Brauchitsch in the W25C Mercedes at the Eifelrennen in 1936. Signed by him at Gräfenwarth in 1993.

to win the German Grand Prix in his Alfa Romeo after von Brauchitsch's car had shed a tyre on the last lap and Hans Stuck took first place in the German Grand Prix for Auto Union, but all the other races went to Mercedes Benz.

In 1936 the C-Type Auto Union was given a 6-litre engine while the engine in the Mercedes was further enlarged to 4.7 litres. The W25A had a shorter wheel base which proved to be difficult for the drivers to handle at speed and so the team was withdrawn for the latter part of the year. Caracciola won in Monaco and Tunis while Nuvolari in his Alfa Romeo claimed the honours at the Eifelrennen. Every other event that year was won by the Auto Union of Bernd Rosemeyer.

W125 Mercedes Benz

In 1937 the entirely new W125 was produced by Mercedes Benz, designed and developed by Rudoph UIhenhaut, with an eight cylinder engine of 5.66 litres. It could produce wheel spin in top gear at 180 mph! Rosemeyer won four races with his Auto Union but Caracciola, Lang and von Brauchitsch between them won nine in the W125.

Manfred Von Brauchitsch in the W125 Mercedes in the Coppa Acerbo, Pescara in 1937.

Manfred Von Brauchitsch leaping over Melbourne Rise in his W125 Mercedes in 1937.

In 1938 the cars had to conform to an entirely new Formula with either 3-litre supercharged or 4.5-litre unsupercharged engines and weighing a minimum of 850 kg. Both German teams chose the supercharged option. The new D Type Auto Union was designed by Dr Robert Eberan von Eberhorst as Ferdinand Porsche was by then occupied in developing the engine of Hitler's "People's Car." It had a V12 engine, situated again behind the driver, and pannier fuel tanks placed on each side of the driver. Sadly Bernd Rosemeyer was killed during a record attempt on the Frankfurt to Darmstadt autobahn when his fully streamlined Auto Union was swept off the road by a strong side wind. It deeply affected the team and there was even a possibility that Auto Union would withdraw from racing altogether. However Nuvolari took Rosemeyer's place and won the last two races of the 1938 season at Monza and Donington Park.

W154 Mercedes Benz

The W154 3-litre Mercedes revved faster than the W125 and, because it consumed a gallon of fuel every two miles, an extra fuel tank was placed more or less over the driver's lap. It made the possibility of fire even more terrifying. The car was heavier than its predecessor but, contrary to expectation, almost as quick. The 1938 Season began at Pau where Rene Dreyfus had a surprise victory in his ugly, underpowered, but less thirsty 4.5-litre unsupercharged Delahaye. Lang, von Brauchitsch and Seaman shared between them the remaining six events.

By this time Mercedes were putting greater resources into motor racing than Auto Union and a rebodied W154/163 car was equipped with a two-stage supercharger. It was lighter and developed 480 bhp at 7500 rpm. It looked even more purposeful with its sleek uncluttered lines. Every race that year was won by the Silver Arrows, six by Mercedes Benz and two by Auto Unions, and five of them were won by Hermann Lang.

The Tripoli Grand Prix in 1939 was restricted to 1.5-litre supercharged cars as the Italians were confident that this would provide a certain win for one of their cars. They were disappointed because Mercedes secretly produced two 1.5-litre cars, designated the W165s, in the space of six months, and with them Lang and Caracciola secured the first two places.

Hermann Muller's D-Type Auto Union harried by two W154 Mercedes at Donington in 1938.

The Death of Dick Seaman

1939 was marred by the death of Dick Seaman who crashed in heavy rain during the Belgian Grand Prix at Spa, his car wrapping itself around a tree and catching fire. Seaman died later in hospital from his burns after admitting, with typical honesty, that it had been his fault as he had been driving too fast.

The Italian Cars

Some might wonder how the thirties could be described as fun years when they were dominated by two teams which outclassed all the others. Well the hundreds of thousands of spectators were entertained by the sight, sound and sheer speed of the cars, and what enthusiast would refuse the opportunity to see those races re-enacted again today! In addition, not all the attention was focused upon the Germans. Mussolini was as anxious as Hitler to see his cars win and the Italian cars added great interest to the races. Enzo Ferrari managed the Alfa Romeo team which sported the yellow shield with its rampant horse that would be carried on all his Ferraris after the war.

Maserati V4

The Maserati brothers had produced the "Seici Cilindri" in 1929 by joining together two eight-cylinder 2-litre engines on a common crankcase with two superchargers and called the V4. A larger version, known as the V5 appeared in 1932 with a 4.9-litre engine and Piero Taruffi drove a development of it at Tripoli in 1934.

Alfa Romeos Tipo A and Tipo B

For 1931 Alfa Romeo Vittorio Jano mounted two six-cylinder supercharged engines, each of 1750cc side by side beneath the bonnet of their Tipo A "Bimotore". The car's engines were increased to 3500cc and, in the hands of Nuvolari, saw action against the Silver Arrows. It had two clutches which were operated together, two gear levers, either of which operated both gearboxes, and two final drives.

Tipo B Alfa Romeo.

12C Alfa Romeo.

Then there was the Alfa Romeo Tipo B which first appeared in 1932 and took the place of the two seater "Monza". For the new Formula in 1934 the Tipo B had an enlarged straight eight 2,905cc engine and this was further increased to 3,822cc in 1935. Nuvolai beat the Mercedes and Auto Unions with this to win the German Grand Prix that year.

In 1936 Alfa Romeo introduced the 12C, an entirely new car with independent suspension on all four wheels, a streamlined body and a V12 4-litre supercharged engine.

The Alfetta

Finally, in 1938, the 1.5-litre supercharged Alfetta arrived, designed by Gioacchino Columbo with a straight 8 cylinder engine. It was confidently expected that that it would win the Tripoli Grand Prix for voiturette cars in 1939 until Mercedes Benz sprang a surprise by producing the two W165 cars which proceeded to dominate the race. However the Alfettas were hidden in a cheese factory for the course of the war and emerged afterwards as the 158 Alfa Romeo's which were supreme in Formula One until they were bettered by Gonzales 4.5-litre Ferrari at Silverstone in 1951.

The Maserati 6C

In 1936 the Maserati brothers produced a six cylinder 1.5 supercharged car for voiturette races to compete with the British E.R.A.s, and this was succeeded by a 4CL powered by a overhead camshaft four cylinder engine with four valves per cylinder. After the war the engine was put into a tubular chassis and became the 4CLT.

The Maserati 8C

Maserati's 3-litre supercharged 8 cylinder car was called the 8C. It had enormous potential and Count Carlo Felice Trossio took the lead ahead of three Mercedes Benz at Livorno in 1938, dropping out with brake problems after eight laps. Paul Pietsch led the German Grand Prix with an 8C at the Nurburgring in 1939. George Monkhouse in *Mercedes Benz Grand Prix Racing 1934–1955* wrote, *"A welcome splash of red amidst the preponderant silver came from ex-Auto Union driver Paul Pietsch's 3 litre works Maserati, holding fourth place on lap one, and pushing into second place behind Lang on round 2! Sensation now followed when Lang had to stop for a plug change, and the Maserati took the lead! – until Pietsch also had to pull in for front brake adjustments, dropping back to fourth behind Nuvolari, Muller and Caracciola."* The Maserati eventually finished in third place behind Caracciola and Muller.

Had Alfa Romeo and Maserati enjoyed the same financial resources as the German teams, and been as well organised, the results of the races in the "Golden Age" might have been very different.

Delahaye and Talbot

The honour of representing France in Grand Prix racing passed from Bugatti to Talbot and Delahaye and, in contrast to the other teams, they chose the 4.5-litre unsupercharged option in 1938.
The Delahaye with which Rene Dreyfus won the Pau Grand Prix in 1938 was an ugly car with a
body that could accommodate two seats so that it could also be used in sports car races. It lacked

(Left) 8C Maserati.

(Right) Luigi Villoresi's 8C Maserati at Pescara in 1938.

the power of its German and Italian rivals but Rene Dreyfus also brought it home to fourth place in the 1939 Mille Miglia.

Talbot re-entered Grand Prix racing in the French Grand Prix of 1938 with a stripped down version of a car that had been successful in sports car races. Ian Connell raced it with considerable success at Brooklands. It had a 4-litre engine and was the brainchild of Tony Lago who was in charge of Talbot-Darracq. He built a single seater Grand Prix car for 1939 with the six cylinder engine enlarged to 4.5 litres and a five-speed gear box. It looked every inch a sleek and powerful contender and Raymond Mays drove it at Spa in the race that cost Seaman his life. Mays was forced to retire with a split fuel tank but later that year Talbot-Darracqs finished third and fourth in the French Grand Prix.

After the war Tony Lago produced the 4.5-litre unsupercharged Lago Talbot. It was not as fast as the 158 Alfas but, consuming less fuel, spent less time in the pits, and this enabled Louis Rosier to win the Belgian Grand Prix in 1948.

The Lago Talbots added greatly to the interest of Grand Prix racing in the late 1940s and Duncan Hamilton had a great affection for them.

Dr Ferry Porsche

Dr. Ferry Porsche, Professor Ferdinand Porsche's son, was closely involved with the design and development of Auto Union racing cars from the beginning. The two decided that most of the weight should be over the rear wheels and so that was where they placed the engine. They also saw the virtue of placing the fuel tank in the middle of the car so that the weight distribution would remain the same right throughout each race. At an early stage in the development of the first 16 cylinder car problems arose with regard to the crankshaft. Ferry suggested that it was because the crankshaft and the crankcase were made of different metals which expanded at different rates. This diagnosis led to the solution of the problem and also solved that of the superchargers tending to overheat. Ferry was the first to drive the A Type car fresh from the factory and

Dr Ferry Porche and Bernd Rosemeyer's Auto Union at the Eifelrennen in 1936.

he took over the development of the cars when his father's attention was transferred to the Volkswagen. In 1935 he solved the problem of the inside rear wheels spinning when cornering by fitting a limited-slip differential. No one at Mercedes could understand why the cars were so improved! Having eventually left Auto Union, Ferry Porsche and his father developed the W154 Mercedes at the end of 1938 so that, designated the W154/163, it was both lighter and more powerful. Ferry believed that one of Mercedes Benz greatest assets was Alfred Neubauer their Team Manager, although Rudolf Uhlenhaut was not so impressed by him.

In 1987 I sent Dr Ferry Porsche a painting of Achille Varzi driving an Auto Union in the 1936 Coppa Acerbo while being pursued by Tazio Nuvolari's Alfa Romeo. I relished an excuse to paint the scene. He wrote:

> *"Many thanks for the beautiful picture. I am delighted with it and shall add it to my collection. I am also delighted at your great interest in the history of racing in the thirties."*

In *Racing the Silver Arrows* by Chris Nixon, Dr Ferry Porsche recorded how, after Professor Eberan-Eberhorst took over at Auto Union, he and his father went to Mercedes Benz. In addition to developing the supercharger for the 1939 W154/163 cars they designed the Mercedes Land Speed Record Car which was prevented from running by the outbreak of war.

Rudolf Uhlenhaut

After sending a painting of Manfred's W125 in the Copper Acerbo in 1937 to Rudolf Uhlenhaut in 1985 he wrote:

> *"Thank you very much for sending the painting of the Mercedes Benz Type 125 racing car. It is an unqualified success: perfect in its dimensions; and looking at the picture, one gets a real feeling of the power of this particular racing car.*
>
> *Although the actual event now lies back 49 years, I can still recall clearly many details.*
>
> *Of each relevant type of the complete Daimler racing stable at least one example has survived, and that in perfect condition and ready for the road. These cars will be shown in our Museum which is currently being extended and modernised in readiness for the One Hundred Years Anniversary of our House. The Museum will be open again from March 1986 and it would be a great pleasure to welcome you here too.*
>
> *I have been in retirement now since 1979 and have reached the age of 79; but, thank goodness, I am still in pretty good shape and my interest in cars is as strong as ever."*

Rudolf Uhlenhaut and the W154 Mercedes Benz.

Sadly I never found an opportunity to get to Stuttgart to meet him and, after sending a further painting, I received the following reply:

> *Dear Revd Bryan,*
>
> *Many thanks for the painting of the Caracciola Mercedes Benz racing car and the portrait of me.*
>
> *My wife was especially delighted with the portrait. She thinks the likeness excellent! Of course, with my 82 years I don't quite look like that any more.*
>
> *Your painting reached us here in Stuttgart just before we are off, once again for Malta, where we have our sailing boat.*
>
> *Some time in the future I would be most delighted to welcome you in Stuttgart and to take you on a tour of the Museum.*
>
> *With kind regards,*
>
> *Yours sincerely,   Rudolf Uhlenhaut.*

Rudolf Uhlenhaut always wrote to me by hand in German as I naturally wrote to him in that language. I later learned that his wife was English and that he was of course fluent in English too!"

Rene Dreyfus

Rene Dreyfus had the distinction of beating the W154 Mercedes Benz of Caracciola and Lang in the 1938 Pau Grand Prix in his Delahaye. Being a Frenchman with a Jewish name it meant a great deal to him. His win was immensely popular with the French crowd and in 1938 he became the National Champion of France.

George Monkhouse described Dreyfus as *"polished, unobtrusive and underrated"*. He drove for both Ettore Bugatti and Enzo Ferrari, describing the first as imperious and the second as impenetrable. In addition to Bugattis and Alfa Romeos, he drove Maseratis and the Delahaye throughout the 1930s with considerable success. In 1940 he was granted leave by the French

Rene Dreyfus overtaking Lang's Mercedes to win the Pau Grand Prix in his Delahaye in 1938.

Government to go to the United States to represent France in the Indianapolis 500 Race driving a 3-litre Maserati. While he was there Germany invaded Paris so Rene could not return until, having joined the United States Army, he took part in its liberation as a Master Sergeant.

After the war he became a gourmet restaurateur with "Le Chanteclair" in New York and it became a focal point for racing drivers from all over the world.

In January 1992 I sent Rene a painting of the Pau Grand Prix and he replied as follows:

> *Dear Revd Apps,*
>
> *I was surprised and most pleased to receive your wonderful painting. It describes so well the start of the Pau Grand Prix which I won with great pride in 1938.*
>
> *Your interest in pre-war racing has impressed me so much that instead of answering all the questions of your letter I am sending you by separate mail* My Two Lives, *a book written by Beverly Kimes and myself and published in 1984.*
>
> *In our book you will be able to get the answers of some of your questions, and live with us a period of racing so different from the racing of today.*
>
> *I am now 87 years old, but I assure you that during the years left to me I will with love look at your marvellous work of art and the thoughts that came with it.*
>
> *With many thanks, I am*
> *Very sincerely,*
> *Rene Dreyfus.*

In August 1992 I sent to Rene a further painting which included a portrait and views of his Bugatti and very powerful 12C-36 Alfa Romeo.

Rene Dreyfus with his Bugatti and Alfa Romeo.

He wrote:

> *"Yes, you have done a marvellous job with the cars and in particular with the face of 'that' young man. When I have visitors in my little studio the first thing they notice now is your painting. It looks as if I am going to get out of the painting and talk to them. The painting of my victory at Monaco by Walther Gotschke is second to it now.*
>
> *To answer your question, I always liked the cars I was racing, with the exception of my two unfortunate years with Maserati in 1931 and 1932.*
>
> *Again all my congratulations for your artful realisation and many, many thanks*
> *Very sincerely and gratefully, Rene*

Rene Dreyfus died 1993 and Beverley Kimes, who was the editor of the publications of the Classic Car Club of America, invited me to a celebration of his life at the University Club 1 West Fifty-Fourth Street New York held on January 22nd 1994. She said, *"Rene talked of you often and of course proudly showed me the paintings you gave to him."*

My signed copy of *My Two Lives* is a reminder of a great period of motor racing and of one who drove some of the most fabulous Grand Prix racing cars of all time.

George Monkhouse

George Monkhouse left a pictorial record of this Golden Age of motor racing since, working as a photographer for Kodak in the 1930s, he accompanied the Mercedes Benz team from race to race. Kath and I had lunch with George and Constance Monkhouse at their flat in Hamble in 1985 and he gave me an original photograph of Onofre Marimon driving his works 250F Maserati in practice for the 1954 German Grand Prix at the Nurburgring the lap before his fatal crash.

Painting of Caracciola's W154 Mercedes at Livorno in 1938 presented to George Monkhouse in 1985.

Later he wrote: *"We enjoyed seeing the Australian Grand Prix on the television and have just received the local Adelaide papers giving all the details. It was hard to recognise the Adelaide that we know and like so much."*

Manfred von Brauchitsch

Manfred von Brauchitsch was known as "Der Pechvogel" or "Unlucky Bird" because although he won some notable races he also lost others when they looked to be securely within his grasp.

He was not generally regarded as having quite as much natural talent as Rudolf Caracciola and Hermann Lang, but he could be as fast as them and he was by far the most spectacular of the three. He was hard on his tyres, brakes and gears and flew higher off the ground at Donington Park than any other driver. He was a passionate driver and wept when his W25 Mercedes shed a tyre on the last lap of the German Grand Prix in 1935 when he was far ahead of the field.

Manfred was a Prussian aristocrat who grew up in a castle. His uncle was a Field Marshall and the Commander of the German Army during the Second World War. Manfred himself was not a Nazi and told me that he looked upon the period of the Empire before 1918 as "the good old days". Yet it was he who succeeded in persuading Hitler in 1931 to grant financial help to Mercedes Benz to aid their efforts in producing world beating racing cars. Murray Walker once told me that he thought von Brauchitsch was a snob and said that he hoped I would be able to reassure him that he wasn't, but I am not entirely sure that Manfred would have wanted to deny the charge! Chris Nixon in his book *Racing the Silver Arrows* has a photograph of the Mercedes Team signing up for the 1934 French Grand Prix and beneath it he wrote that *"the aristocratic Manfred von Brauchitsch seems to be regarding the unshaven Fagioli with some contempt."* Both he and Rudolf Caracciola were opposed to Hermann Lang rising from the lowly ranks of a mechanic to join the team of drivers, and he once told me with some pride that the priest who preached at the ceremony of his Confirmation was the Senior Court Chaplain to Emperor William II. An old injury from a motorcycle race kept him from active service in the war and afterwards he fled to East Germany where he eventually became the President of the East German Olympic Team.

The "Silberpfeile"

Manfred first rose to fame in 1932 when he had a stream-lined body fitted to his cousin's SSKL Mercedes Benz and won the Avus Grand Prix, beating Caracciola in a works car. The modified SSKL clearly influenced the design of the W25 which he was asked to drive in its first race in 1934. He won that race after the Italian Luigi Fagioli, on being asked to slow down to enable his German team mate to win, parked his car on the circuit in disgust! Before the race it was discovered that the new cars were too heavy to conform to the 750 kg limit and it was Manfred who suggested that the paint should be stripped off to reduce their weight. As a result the W25s ran with

Manfred Von Brauchitsch in the 1930s.

their aluminium bodies exposed and it was decided that from henceforth silver and not white should be the racing colour of Germany. It was in this way that the "Silberpfeils" or "Silver Arrows" were born. Manfred drove the "Silberpfeils" from 1934 until 1939, winning the Monaco Grand Prix in 1937 with the W125 and the French Grand Prix in 1938 with the W154. His car caught fire in the pits during the German Grand Prix in 1938 while it was being refuelled. When the fire

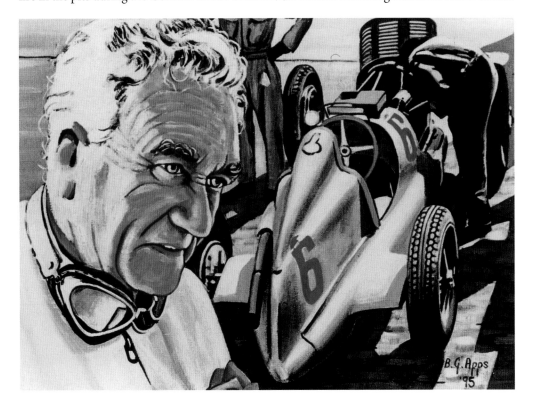

Manfred Von Brauchitsch and the W25 Mercedes.

Manfred Von Brauchitsch's
W125 Mercedes proving difficult to start after a pit stop, in
the Coppa Acerbo in 1937.

had been extinguished he returned to the race with his car still covered in foam, but walked back soon afterwards holding its steering wheel. It had come off in his hands at a point in the course where the car leapt from the ground at great speed! Incidentally Jackie Stewart has said that his B.R.M. would leap from the Nurburgring circuit thirteen times each lap!

Manfred von Brauchitsch eventually became the last of the really great drivers from the 1930s and, living deep in a forested area of Eastern Germany, he had few visitors.

When I first wrote to von Brauchitsch I sent him a painting of him driving the W25 car in its first race. He was delighted with the gift, and a regular correspondence followed during which I sent him a number of other paintings. When he received a painting of the 1937 Donington Grand Prix he wrote, *"This picture of Donington is to be regarded as a remembrance of my life at that time, as a particular bright shining diamond. It really was a battle for one's life in the superlative, to slide around curves for hours on end in my skidding car (nearly always under control) at high speeds at greatest risk! And to drive in front until three laps before the end of the race when my tyre burst – tyre change – and with that, Rosemeyer was the winner."* He really enjoyed his motor racing! I once asked him whom he thought was the best of the Auto Union drivers and I was not surprised when his reply was *"Rosemeyer was number one and the only opponent for Caracciola and me. The team rivalry was great so I never drove an Auto Union car."*

He approved of my painting of the 1937 Monaco Grand Prix, *"showing the fight between Caracciola and myself on the last bend to decide the winner. You really did succeed in catching and pinpointing the finest details of the battle and tension between two drivers where metres and seconds were precious in this contest."* He added, *"In my thoughts I stroll along with you for that lovely walk along the beach. Our common bond to nature is so visible with the respect and friendship we share."*

When I sent him a painting of the W154/163 car he wrote, *"We must talk to each other one day personally. By the way I think about this 'murder tool' (meaning the W154/163 Mercedes) with absolutely no affection.*

May God give you health and strength, joy of life, contentment and a deep gratitude that life is filled with true happiness."

Manfred told me of how his hands would blister and bleed as he handled these great cars with their narrow wheels over demanding road circuits like the Nurburgring for many more miles than are required by a modern Grand Prix. He wore special shoes with soles of leather and asbestos to withstand the heat from the engine but only a thin leather helmet on his head. There were curbs, trees and houses lining the circuits and no room for mistakes.

Our visit to Gräfenwarth

When, in 1993, Kath, Michael and I met Manfred in his home in Gräfenwarth his wife Lieselotte said that they no longer travelled anywhere because people would come up and say "we thought you were dead!" In meeting him, I recalled the old copies of *Motor Sport* I had come across as a boy containing photographs of him racing in the Donington Park Grands Prix. He had booked us into the Hotel Luginsland near his home and said that he would meet us there on the morning after we had arrived and had time to refresh ourselves. As I stepped out of the hotel at nine o'clock the next day Manfred and Lieselotte drew up in a large maroon Mercedes which contrasted sharply with the Trabants that otherwise occupied all the roads. Maroon of course had been the colour of his racing helmet. We met as old friends and were welcomed most warmly. They drove us back to their house while I marvelled at being driven by the great von Brauchitsch. Lieselotte, who sat in the back with Kath and Michael, warned him to remember that he was *"not Manfred*

Manfred Von Brauchitsch with No. 54 at Livorno and No. 26 at Rheims. Both in 1938.

(Left) Manfred at home with photographs of his days with Mercedes Benz.

(Below) One of the paintings by the author.

Lieselotte and Manfred in
their garden with Kath and I.

the racer now!" As we drove into the grounds of their home he said, "Here Manfred is king" and, once inside, I saw all the paintings I had sent him displayed on the walls of the entrance hall and lounge. He gave me prints by Nicholas Watts of his victories at Monaco and Rheims and I in turn gave him my portrait of himself, which prompted a toast accompanied by a smart clicking of heels! By a strange coincidence, Kath and Lieselotte exchanged gifts of artificial flower arrangements. We were guided through an enormous photograph album which illustrated Manfred's years as a racing driver and featured all the interesting people they had met. Then we were taken back to the hotel for lunch and Lieselotte was anxious to see how we liked the Thuringian potatoes. They both rested in the afternoon and we were taken on a tour of the region by a man whom they employed. After this we rejoined them for an evening meal and chatted well into the night. Manfred's English was about as good as my German, but Lieselotte spoke excellent English and so language did not present a problem.

On January 1st 2001 he wrote *"I keep the photo of my English friend Bryan in my motor racing album. I am sorry for my long silence but I suffered a few strokes in May, which took away the necessary horse-power! In the meantime I have refuelled again and am getting back to full power! Thank God for that!"*

Later in 2001 he was delighted with a further painting I had sent of his W125 at Donington and wrote the following: *"It stands on the mantelpiece for everyone to see – that's the place of honour!"* He would end his letters with *"to my friend on the coast from your racing friend in the forest."*

A Letter from Lieselotte

Then I had a letter from Lieselotte dated December 24th 2002 in which she wrote, *"Don't be surprised that I write and give you a big 'thank you' for this beautiful painting which gave us great pleasure. But I feel I should tell you that my husband is not always able to write to you. He has had four strokes and has not fully recovered from that. It is a constant fluctuation between illness and recovery. However we are optimistic and have to be patient."*

Manfred passed away on February 5th 2003 aged 97 and I first received the news when I picked up an invitation from Lieselotte to his funeral service which was to be held at 11a.m. on February 12th. The invitation had been lying on the door mat at the vicarage for some days because, having recently retired, I no longer lived there. Calling to collect any post that was waiting for me I realised that I had come upon it at precisely 11a.m. on the 12th and that the service in Germany had just begun. Lieselotte later sent me a photograph of his grave which was covered with great floral tributes and had his W125 Mercedes etched into the stone. She wrote that many hundreds of people came along to his funeral. She was almost blind and told me, *"As before, I can neither read nor write but I am looked after by dear Kerstin who has been with me for the past ten years."* Later in

Manfred with Mika Hakkinen
and David Coulthard.

the year she sent me a year book entitled *Hematjahrbuch 2004 des Saale-Orla-Kreises* which contained an illustrated article about Manfred.

Then finally I had a letter dated March 9th, 2004 from her housekeeper to say that Lieselotte too had died. She wrote, *"The couple valued your friendship very much and followed the happenings in your family with great interest. They often spoke about you. It is sad that they are no longer with us. They were indeed an enrichment in my life and in your life too, I believe. I would like to thank you for giving them so much support and comfort. You were a valued and important person in their lives. Some of your paintings are now on show in the Mercedes Benz Museum in Stuttgart. All good wishes, and, more importantly, good health, to you and your family from Kerstin Dietzsch.*

Hermann Lang

Hermann Lang first joined the Mercedes Benz Racing Department as a mechanic and engine fitter, and he was transferred to their Test Department in 1934. He became a reserve driver for the racing team when first Krauss and then Neubauer spotted his potential. He was Fagioli's mechanic but was asked to compete in the Eifel race in 1935 in which he finished fifth, the highest placed Mercedes driver. Lang found that his previous experience in racing motorbikes with side cars helped him, as the driving characteristics required in both cases were similar. With growing experience he found that he could soon compete with Caracciola and von Brauchitsch on equal terms although these other drivers resented the fact that a mere mechanic had been promoted in this way. He had to prove himself by his driving skills alone without fear or favour, and he more than justified his place with the other two Germans and the talented British driver Dick Seaman. Lang turned down an offer from Ferdinand Porsche to drive for Auto Union at the end of 1936 and instead drove the W125 Mercedes with its 5.7-litre supercharged engine. The cars were fitted with streamlined bodies enclosing their wheels for the banked Avus circuit and Lang found that the covers over the front wheels produced cushion of air underneath the cars that lifted them off the ground. The covers were removed and Lang won the race after both Caracciola and von Brauchitsch had retired. He also won the Tripoli Grand Prix that year. He had a bad crash in 1937 when his car left the road in the Masaryk Grand Prix in Czechoslovakia, killing two spectators and injuring twelve others. Then a broken shock absorber cost him the race at Donington Park. For 1938 Mercedes fielded the 3-litre supercharged W154s. He won the Tripoli Grand Prix again and was third at Rheims. He was second to Dick Seaman in the German Grand Prix, and won the race at Livorno after von Brauchitsch had been disqualified for receiving outside assistance. At Pescara he had to abandon his burning car and was given a lift back to the pits by Rene Dreyfus in his Delahaye. At Donington in 1938 Lang was robbed of victory when a stone shattered his windshield, but 1939 was Lang's year. He won the Pau, Tripoli, Eifel, Belgian and Swiss Grands Prix. However he could derive no pleasure from winning the Belgian event because it was during the course of that race that Dick Seaman crashed off the course and into a tree. His car caught fire

Signed photograph of Hermann Lang.

Hermann Lang winning the hill climb at Grosslockner to become European Mountain champion in 1939.

Hermann Lang's W125
Mercedes in the pits during
the German Grand Prix in
1937.

and he later died in hospital as a result of his burns. After the war Lang won the Le Mans race in 1952 in the 300SL Mercedes with gull wing doors.

He wrote to me in 1987, after I had sent him paintings of him driving the W125 and W154 Mercedes in the 1930s and he also sent me some signed photographs of himself and his cars.

9 January 1987.

Dear Reverend Apps,

Many thanks for your letters of 12 December 1985 and 11 November 1986 respectively.

My two sons and I are delighted with both your paintings which are prominently displayed in our home. You have succeeded in capturing the car, and also the person, extremely well. My most sincere thanks.

What time and trouble it must have taken you firstly, to re-create in your mind's eye a racing event of so long ago, and then to recapture it onto canvas! Well, with your special feeling for the subject and your dedicated application you have succeeded admirably. You have my unbounded admiration.

Before the Second World War all racing events – and especially the Grands Prix – were truly enjoyable not only for those racing, but also for the crowds, as I have been told often times since. Hundreds of thousands of enthusiastic spectators witnessed the 'Eifel Races' and the 'Grand Prix' events on the Nurburgring; and those who once had experienced any of these events in Germany never missed them again. The spectators also had the opportunity to actually observe the drivers during their training sessions and the races, as in those days we only wore close fitting caps and light coloured goggles. Nowadays the drivers are completely concealed in their vehicles and can really only be seen at the distribution of the prizes.

I beg you to forgive this rather late reply to your kind letters.

My wife's and my own illnesses have, unfortunately, compelled us to make many changes

Hermann Lang winning the Eifel Grand Prix at the Nurburgring in 1939.

to our daily lives. We both are not what we used to be; and so even letters such as yours remain unanswered for a long time. Please try to understand.

For your records I have enclosed an autographed photograph of the days from before the Second World War and also a more recent one in gratitude and appreciation of your keen interest in these particular racing seasons.

With best regards,
Hermann Lang

Hermann Lang passed away later that year on October 19th at the age of 78. In the December issue of *Motor Sport* it said that he had been virtually unbeatable in 1939 and had become the yardstick for others to try to beat, winning five of the eight major Grand Prix races with the 3-litre V12 Mercedes Benz.

Signed photograph of Hermann Lang returning to his W125 Mercedes after the war.

ENZO FERRARI

IN *ENZO FERRARI the Man* Gino Rancati wrote that it had been said of him that he was *"malicious, witty, subtly argumentative, hostile or friendly depending on the moment, stubborn with an unyielding courage, and with an almost prophetic spirit."* Clearly Enzo Ferrari had a complicated personality that defied any simple definition. One facet of his nature was revealed by his mechanics who are reputed to have said, *"It's a pity that Enzo Ferrari isn't the Pope, because if he was we would only have to kiss his ring!"* Ferrari was certainly unique and he could be formidable. He was never present at a race in which his cars competed, saying that his nerves couldn't stand it, and I wonder if it was because he feared for the safety of his drivers. Certainly a number of his drivers died at the wheel and he was twice threatened with charges of manslaughter. After the fatal crashes of Alfonso de Portago and Wolfgang von Trips, both of which also cost the lives of spectators, the press unfairly accused Ferrari of killing people, but he was not an uncaring man and visited the grave of his son Dino, who had died at the age of twenty-four from muscular dystrophy, every morning until he himself died.

The Racing Driver

Having caught the motor racing bug at the age of ten when he was taken to a race by his father, Alfredo, Enzo began racing in 1919 and remained at the very heart of motor sport right up to his death at the age of ninety on 14th August 1988. I always thought that it was hard to imagine the sport without him and motor racing has never been quite the same since he has gone.

He took part in the Targa Florio in 1919 and again the following year when he drove an Alfa Romeo into second place.

In 1923 he won the Circuito del Savio at Ravenna and as a result of this Count Enrico Baracca, the father of Francesco, a hero of the First World War, asked him to display on his cars the squadron badge of his late son who was a hero of the First World War to bring him luck. It was of course the Il Cavallino Rampante and Enzo added the yellow background because this was the colour of Modena.

In 1924 he won the Coppa Acerbo in Pescara, again driving an Alfa Romeo. After Guiseppe Campari had been forced to retire in his P2 Alfa, Enzo roundly defeated the works Mercedes cars.

Scuderia Ferrari

Enzo gave up racing in 1932 after the birth of his son Dino, believing that it would have been irresponsible to continue to race when he was a father. In the absence of a works Alfa Romeo team he had established Scuderia Ferrari in 1929 to support private owners of Alfa Romeos. Giuseppe Campari and Tazio Nuvolari were amongst those who signed up to an arrangement by which, while they were unpaid, they received a portion of the prize money.

Alfa Romeo fully supported Scuderia Ferrari so that it became the works team. Enzo was supplied with six P3s to take on the mighty Silver Arrows of Germany and he produced the immensely powerful twin-engined Bimotore. Rene Dreyfus became one of his drivers but Nuvolari eventually left him to drive for Auto Union.

Ferrari was responsible for building the 1.5-litre supercharged Alfetta which was later to become the 158 Alfa Romeo but at the end of the 1930s his status was reduced to that of a Team Manager at Alfa Romeo. He considered this to be intolerable and so left Alfa Romeo to produce his own car. Disallowed by Alfa Romeo from using his own name he simply called it 815, indicating that it was an 8 cylinder car of 1.5 litres. It took part in the 1940 Mille Miglia.

A Grand Prix Ferrari

After the War Enzo produced the first Grand Prix Ferrari, the V12 1.5-litre supercharged Tipo 125, designed by Colombo. He loved powerful engines and used to say that streamlining was for those who couldn't build them. Then came the V12 4.5-litre unsupercharged car which, to his enormous satisfaction, beat the 158 Alfa Romeo of Juan Fangio to win the British Grand Prix at Silverstone in the hands of Froilan Gonzales.

Froilan Gonzales winning the British Grand Prix at Silverstone in the 4.5-litre Ferrari in 1951.

Following the withdrawal of Alfa Romeo at the end of 1951, Formula One was restricted to 2-litre unsupercharged cars. It included the British Cooper Bristols and H.W.M.s but Alberto Ascari won the World Championship in both 1952 and 1953 in the 4-cylinder Ferrari Tipo 500 designed by Lampredi. The impressive return of Mercedes Benz in 1954 eclipsed the Italian cars for two years and, after this, Ferrari shared the honours with Maserati and Vanwall, Fangio winning the World Championship for Ferrari in 1956 with the V8 Lancia D50s which had been entrusted to Ferrari's care.

Alberto Ascari winning the Dutch Grand Prix in 1952 with his 2-litre unsupercharged Ferrari Tipo 500.

Mike Hawthorn won the World Championship for Enzo Ferrari in 1958 with the Lancia Ferrari and Phil Hill took the Championship for him in 1961 with the shark-nosed rear-engine car. While phoning me from the United States, Phil Hill told me that Enzo had ordered all the 1961 cars to be broken up after a dispute with the Italian Government.

Between them, John Surtees and Niki Lauda gained the title for Ferrari in 1964, 1977 and 1979 and the World Constructor's Championship was won by Ferrari in 1982 and 1983 but it was only after the death of the great man that Michael Schumacher brought back the glory days to the stable.

Ferrari was of course highly successful in sports car races at Le Mans and elsewhere.

A number of drivers lost their lives driving for Ferrari and Gino Rancati records that he said, *"I am continually afflicted by an inner suffering and when*

I entrust a car to a driver and shake his hand in the courtyard, I always think that perhaps I will be attending his funeral in a few days time." He went on to add, *"Enthusiasm and passion, not profit or ambition, are the driving forced behind racing drivers and manufacturers of racing cars."*

Murray Walker wrote in *Formula One Heroes*, *"If I had to name one individual as the greatest of all in the history of motor sport, I would without a moment's hesitation nominate Enzo Ferrari."*

My Correspondence with Enzo Ferrari

I was of the same opinion when in 1985 I sent Enzo Ferrari a painting of Alberto Ascari winning the British Grand Prix in 1952, and I was thrilled to receive the following postcard written in Italian and personally signed in his violet ink.

> *Very Reverend Apps,*
> *Thank you for the beautiful painting and for the honour bestowed on me"*
> *Cordial greetings, Ferrari.*
> *Modena, 21/6/1985*

Enzo Ferrari's postcard.

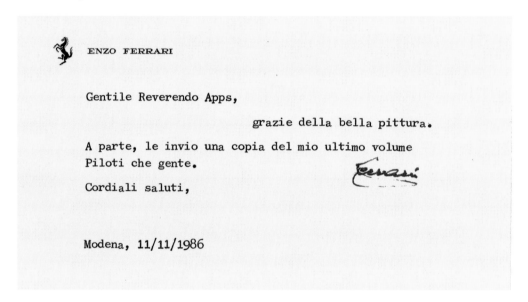

At the end of 1986 I sent Ferrari a painting of Mike Hawthorn winning the French Grand Prix at Rheims in 1958 in the 2.5-litre Ferrari Dino and on 11 November 1986 he wrote to me again, and I was even more delighted with his reply. Thanking me for the painting he said that he had sent me the latest copy of his book *Piloti, Che Gente*.

The book arrived a few days later, wrapped only in a single sheet of thin brown paper but in perfect condition. *The driver and the Man* traced the history of motor racing from the earliest days, with particular emphasise on his own cars and drivers. It was a large volume richly illustrated in colour.

Then at the end of 1987 I posted to Enzo Ferrari a painting of Peter Collins winning the British Grand Prix in the Ferrari Dino 246 in 1958. Tragically Peter Collins had died during the German Grand Prix at the Nurburgring the following month and, with Stirling Moss, Mike Hawthorn and Tony Brooks, Peter Collins was one of the finest British drivers of all time.

Now it so happened that at the end 1987 Ferraris had won the last two races of the season in Japan and Australia. I innocently remarked in my letter that it surely warranted an additional chapter to *Piloti, Che Gente*. To my immense surprise Ferrari wrote the following:

> *Modena 4 dicembre 1987*
> *Dear Reverend Apps,*
> *Thank you for your letter of 23rd November, especially for the beautiful momento of my friend Collins.*
> *In the next few days I shall send you the latest edition of my book* Piloti, Che Gente, *brought up to date with the protagonists of the latest Grands Prix.*
> *Cordial greetings,*
> *Ferrari*

Peter Collins spoke Italian fluently and, in addition, had a personal charm that everyone, and not least, the ladies, tended to find irresistible. It's not surprising therefore that Ferrari should have described Peter as his friend.

The book duly arrived, this time with an illustrated cover and the additional chapter.

Early the next year it was reported in *Motor Sport* that Ferrari had spoken at a recent meeting about the latest edition of his book, and expressed his dismay that someone had sold a signed copy in New York. To him it had been a betrayal of his personal loyalty.

He was asked if he would be marking his birthday by publishing a full autobiography. *"'Perhaps,' he smiled. "I could call it, 'Ferrari: The First 90 Years'."*

Peter Collins winning the British Grand Prix in the Dino 246 Ferrari.

The following August I planned to send a painting to Enzo Ferrari to mark his ninetieth birthday with portraits of him as a young man and in older age, together with various Ferrari racing cars. It had all crystallised in my mind when I stepped on board a cross Channel ferry, bound for a family holiday in France but, buying a newspaper, I saw immediately the announcement of his death. The news had been delayed until after his funeral which, being kept secret according to his wishes, was attended by only six people. It was the end of an era. Between 1947 and 1988 Ferraris had won over five thousand races.

I was determined to produce the painting I had planned and decided to send it to his son Piero Lardi Ferrari who had taken over the management of the racing team. As soon as I was back in Bournemouth I started on the painting and sent it off. Piero Ferrari thanked me for the gift and sent me the further edition of his father's book.

Postscript

An appreciation of Enzo Ferrari by Dennis Jenkinson appeared later in *Motor Sport* which included a reference to the great man's dotage and, while I had a profound admiration for Dennis Jenkinson as a motor racing journalist, I felt that the reference should not be allowed to pass without comment. I wrote that in my recent experience Enzo Ferrari's mind had in no way been impaired by age and the fact that he "doted on racing cars redounded to his praise". My letter appeared in *Motor Sport* the next month.

A tribute to Enzo Ferrari.

RAYMOND MAYS AND THE V16 B.R.M.

MY ONLY regret when I came away from Goodwood in 1949 was that the Italian 4CLT Maserati of Reg Parnell was so much faster than any of the British cars there. Parnell was unofficially anointed as the "King of Goodwood" but he had to drive a foreign car to win that title. Then, not long after that race meeting at Goodwood, I heard of Raymond Mays' project to produce a British car that would beat the world. Raymond Mays and Peter Berthon, who had together been responsible for the creating the E.R.A.s (English Racing Automobiles), before the war, were developing the B.R.M. (British Racing Motor), of an advanced design which looked certain to succeed. They had the backing of the British Motor Industry and, in particular that of two leading industrialists Alfred Owen and Tony Vandervell. Rivers Fletcher organised a supporters club called the B.R.M.A. and my brother David and I became members by subscribing five shillings each. We fondly believed that this would pay for two of the car's sixteen sparking plugs!

The patriotic enthusiasm that accompanied this very British project immediately after the Second World War was exemplified by the reaction of Alfred Owen to the plans of Raymond Mays, which is recorded in *B.R.M.* by Raymond Mays and Peter Roberts. *"He said: 'Well, I'm all for our country. This project of yours is important,' he went on, 'because it is impossible to know where pioneer work like this will lead us. Do you realise, for instance, that it is hardly an exaggeration to say that we owe the existence of this country to Lady Houston? When the Government refused to build machines to fly for the Schneider Trophy, she came forward and put the money down. The research that went into building the Supermarine seaplane which won the trophy outright led, as you know, to the development of the Rolls Royce Merlin engine and the Spitfire fighters.'"*

The story of the B.R.M. is recounted comprehensively in Doug Nye's *B.R.M. - The Saga of British Racing Motors*.

Sadly, the design of the sixteen cylinder cars proved to be too advanced and complex to be fully developed before time was called on the Grand Prix formula for which they were designed. Added to this, the project suffered from being run by a committee, and depending on two hundred different contributors from the motor industry. Eventually Tony Vandervell withdrew his support and built his own cars, while Alfred Owen bought out the whole concern and eventually, with the help of Tony Rudd, made it succeed.

The "Nearly Car."

Back in 1950 I was determined to support the B.R.M. come what may and was undaunted by the fact that in its first race at Silverstone it moved only inches from the starting line before its drive shaft broke!

The V16 was the "nearly car" that in the beginning of the 1950s promised so much only to disappoint again and again. Yet it was an exciting time for a young enthusiast who could see that,

The first B.R.M. in its original form being tested by Ken Richardson.

on paper at least, it was a world beater, and who firmly believed after each failure that next time it might win.

The drama of the 1.5-litre supercharged V16 car was heightened by the fact that its initial races were always preceded by the B.R.M. mechanics working through the night in order to get just one car to the line. Invariably the car started from the back of the grid because it had still been in pieces at Bourne when the other competitors were practicing for the race!

Hailed a World Beater

After winning two short races at Goodwood in September 1950 in the hands of who else but Reg Parnell the *Sunday Express* was ecstatic, proclaiming *"B.R.M. wins: 'This car is a world-beater."* Then, in the Spanish Grand Prix at Barcelona the next month, Parnell overtook no less than seventeen cars on the first lap to run in fourth place. But both he and Peter Walker retired with mechanical problems later in the race and the press, expecting far too much so early in the car's development, was unforgiving. Parnell and Walker finished fifth and seventh in the British Grand Prix the next year, having started once again from the back of the grid, and limiting their engine revs to keep them going to the finish. Both drivers suffered severe burns from excessive heat in their cockpits.

Scorned as Abject Failure

The Italian Grand Prix at Monza followed and the newspaper headlines read *"SNEERS AS BRM CARS FLOP AGAIN"*. The cars were withdrawn before the race after gearbox problems came to light during practice, but Ken Richardson, B.R.M.'s test driver, told me years later that he had reached 12,000 revs per minute on one lap, which represented 203 mph. The cars stayed at Monza to be "tested to destruction" in an effort to iron out all their problems, and the great Fangio drove one at speeds equal to those of the Alfa Romeos and Ferraris. But Monza proved to be the last chance for B.R.M.s to win a major Grand Prix, because in 1952 the 2-litre Formula was adopted instead. Even so, the press did not lose interest in the B.R.M.s and the cars were still capable of making the headlines.

At Albi in 1952 the two B.R.M.s were driven by the Argentinians Juan Fangio and Froilan Gonzales and, after leading the big Ferraris and breaking the lap record, they failed when porous castings let water into their engines. The papers reported, *"B.R.Ms LEAD – BUT THEN DISASTER. They failed again today, those squat little B.R.M.s with which we hoped to beat the motor-racing world. But it was a new kind of failure, almost glorious."*

My B.R.M. Scrap Book

I kept a Scrap Book of the B.R.M. in which I recorded each race with the aid of newspaper cuttings, and in 1952 posted it to Raymond Mays in Bourne, audaciously asking him to write a Foreword for it. He replied on June 10th 1952.

> *"Dear Bryan,*
>
> *Thank you for sending your most interesting letter of 9th and for sending your B.R.M. book. I cannot tell you how much I admire this book and the way in which you have arranged it, and I am very pleased indeed to send you a little Foreword for it. I hope you will excuse this being typewritten but, as you can imagine, I am terribly busy, and also, after all the work and disappointment, I am very tired. The result of Albi and Dundrod, after all the months of preparation, was a crushing disappointment, but we are still hoping that by our showing later in the year at Silverstone and Boreham we may be able to justify our efforts and the faith of our good friend. We are aiming at re-establishing confidence so that we may be able to go ahead with the building of a car for the new Formula.*
>
> *With many thanks for your good wishes, and I am so glad to know of all your interest in the project.*
>
> > *Yours sincerely,*
> > *Raymond Mays.*
>
> *P.S. I am so pleased with your book that I should like to keep it for a day or two to show to my co-directors at the beginning of the week."*

The following is the Foreword which duly arrived and was pasted in the front of the book.

> *"My whole life has been given up to the development of racing cars, and actually racing them. I was the originator of the E.R.A., which won so many races both in England and on the Continent.*
>
> *After the war I was the instigator of the B.R.M. project. The idea at the back of my mind in starting this was to try to produce a national racing car which could uphold British prestige throughout the world in International Grand Prix events."*

I wonder, would a fourteen year old boy's letter be met with such a response from such a person today? But these were the 1950s and that was the way it was in those days.

Signed photograph of Raymond Mays in the V16 B.R.M. in 1952.

Drama on the track

The drama continued on the race track and a Formula Libre race was held at Silverstone on July 17 1952 to enable two B.R.Ms, driven by Froilan Gonzales and Ken Wharton, to get to grips with

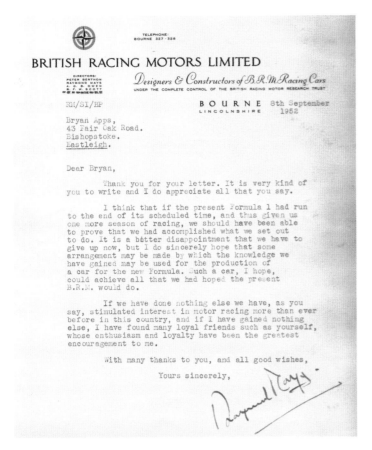

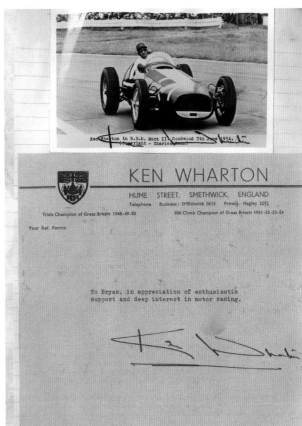

the 4.5-litre Ferraris. There were three Ferraris in the hands of Luigi Villoresi, Chico Landi and Louis Rosier and the "Thinwall Special" Ferrari driven by Piero Taruffi.

The *Daily Express* thundered, *"ONE HUNDRED THOUSAND people at Silverstone yesterday leaped to their feet to see the lime green B.R.M., Britain's jinx car battling the Italians for the lead in a big race. And then – failure."* Taruffi jumped the start so that the real leader was Gonzales, followed by Villoresi and Wharton. Not realising that Taruffi had been penalised, Gonzales went flat out to catch him and, in consequence, limped back to the pits with a large stake impaled in his car's radiator after leaving the circuit at speed! Wharton's car was brought in and the driver was almost pulled out of his seat by Gonzales who was immediately off again, reducing the deficit from 50 to 30 seconds before his gearbox failed and his race was over.

(Left) Letter from Raymond Mays in September 1952.

(Right) Signed photograph of Ken Wharton in the shorter and lighter Mark II B.R.M. in 1954.

Hopes for a New Car

I continued to correspond with Raymond Mays over the years that followed and in this way I was enabled to feel that I was "on the inside" with privileged information.

In September 1952 he wrote that he hoped that the knowledge that they had gained could be used for the production of a car for the new Formula.

Tony Rudd

Tony Rudd joined B.R.M. early on in its history in the V16 days and he was the one most responsible for achieving Graham Hill's World Championship in 1962.

Writing in 1987 Tony Rudd told me, *"Motor racing seems very different now to 1951. We paid Reg Parnell £200 a drive and £2,000 a year retainer, which compares with $3,000,000 for a driver today. We once costed a V16 at £15,000 each which compares with £35,000 for a DFY and £80,000 for a Renault."* He also wrote, *"I have recently spent some time with Tony Merrick and the Montagu Museum V16 and had been over to Donington to help sort out Tom Wheatcroft's Mark II."*

Froilan Gonzales

Gonzales drove the B.R.M. for a few laps at Donington in 1989 during the making of a short film, and he wrote to me afterwards that he was *"very happy to be at Donington that day hearing the wonderful noise of those sixteen cylinders together roaring at speed."*

Juan Fangio

Raymond Mays was fortunate in gaining the services of both Juan Fangio and Froilan Gonzales. Fangio wrote to me in 1985, *"I raced in Ireland with the B.R.M., but as a result of the accident which occurred in Monza in 1952, my contacts with the team came to an end. At that time there were still some things missing, which had considerable importance. Perhaps the fixed supercharger had some influence. Turbo engines have since improved a great deal, as we all know."*

His accident occurred in a non championship event before the beginning of the 1952 season when, crashing on the second lap while driving a Maserati A6GCM, he broke his neck and so missed the whole of that year.

Stirling Moss, who tested the B.R.M. at Monza early on in its development, had a wretched race in Ulster in a car that was ill prepared. He wrote in my copy of Doug Nye's book, *"The 16 cylinder B.R.M. was probably the best sounding worst car I ever drove. The 4 cylinder was great."*

Perhaps the last word here should be given to Rivers Fletcher who wrote the bulletins for the B.R.M.A. and offered this for my book. *"The V16 was much the fastest and most exciting car I ever drove, a fabulous achievement but impractical and ahead of its time in technology and materials. Mays and Berthon are remembered as people who attempted too much but nevertheless achieved a brilliant and memorable racing car."*

Count Giavani Lurani

An interesting incident occurred during the fraught practice sessions before the 1951 Italian Grand Prix. Reg Parnell's B.R.M. having lapped at high speed for several laps, broke a big end and so the mechanics were called upon to work an all night shift again to replace the engine. In the meantime Ken Richardson had gone off the circuit, having been unable to select third gear. There was damage to the front end of the body, the radiator and the steering arm, and Raymond Mays in his book described how Alfa Romeo straightened and tested the steering arm, while his old friend "the charming Count 'Johnny' Lurani" arranged for all the body repairs to be done. It was the kind of situation that wouldn't happen today.

Count Johnny Lurani and his Maserati 4CM.

In 1992 I sent Count Lurani a painting of him driving a 4CM Maserati before the war, together with a portrait of him wearing a red and white cap, and received the following reply.

Signed photograph of Johnny Lurani.

C. TE DOTT. ING. GIOVANNI LURANI CERNUSCHI

My dear Reverend,

Please forgive the long delay in answering to your great gift and your letter. It was addressed to St. Moritz in Switzerland and it reached me only now here in my home address that is in Cerusco (Italy) as you will see on the writing paper.

I was absolutely astonished and extremely happy to get your nice painting and letter. In my extreme age one lives very much with the past and one appreciates particularly the contacts one has with people that still remember you after so many years.

I am very much intrigued and wish to know a few things. First thing how did you find my address and how did it come into your mind to paint such a lovely picture for me. Of all people that your evident knowledge of motor racing has brought to your attention, how did I emerge and be blessed with your kindness and generosity. Your painting must have been taken from the photo that is printed in my early book, "Racing Round the World" and it depicts me when I drove my little Maserati 1100cc 4 cyl. for the first time in the Turin Grand Prix in the spring of 1937 and won the 1100cc division.

I wonder from where you got the idea of painting the head of mine that peeps out from the corner in the white and red hat! I had a cap rather similar at the Rheims Grand Prix (French G. P.) when I was a steward. But it was white and blue!

I am very old. My coming birthday next December will be 87 if I ever reach it! I wish I could meet you. I wish I could invite you here to see my very old house where I was born and I live. And of course very many "automobilia"! I enclose a few Xmas cards of mine so that you can see some of the cars I had (some are still with me of course....) and something of our house.

I would like to send you something that might give you pleasure and show you my gratefulness and the great appreciation of the great present you sent to me. For the moment I beg you to pray for me.

If by chance you can come to Italy you will be my guest here whenever you like and I will take you to the Monza track in any case.

With all my best thanks and good wishes

Yours Johnny Lurani

The painting had found Count Lurani because I had sent it to the B.R.D.C. for them to forward. I had only guessed that his cap was red and white, having to work from a black and white

Count Johnny Lurani and his M.G. in the 1933 Mille Miglia.

photograph. He sent me photographs of some of the interesting cars he owned and one of both him and his wife in his 1910 Lancia outside the imposing wrought iron gates of his chateau near Monza.

As he had been so pleased with the painting of the Maserati I sent a further painting later that year, this time featuring the M.G. Magnette which he drove in the 1933 Mille Miglia with George Eyston. They won the 1100cc class in 18 hours, 1 minute, 40 seconds beating the previous record by 34 minutes. The painting also included a small portrait of him at that earlier stage in his life.

In his *Behind the Scenes*, Louis Stanley wrote that in Count Lurani's stables and garages, past and present merged in a remarkable collection of historic racing cars. *"On one occasion the place was enlivened by a mixture of film stars and racing people, everyone wandering about in evening dress as if about to have dinner when in point of time we had just finished breakfast."*

Sadly I received a letter from his son who said that although his father had had time to appreciate the second painting and to place it near the first one in his study he had since suffered a stroke and so was unable to thank me for it.

Two of the photographs that Count Johnny Lurani sent me.

THE OWEN RACING ORGANISATION

B.R.M. was saved from oblivion by being bought by Rubery Owen in October 1952, and two years later Alfred Owen agreed to write this Foreword for the second volume of my Scrap Book.

Donald Campbell's 'Bluebird' and the 1962 V8 B.R.M. Both built by the Owen Organisation.

I am very pleased to have this opportunity of saying a few brief words about the B.R.M.

From its earliest days I have taken a personal interest in its development, and when so many problems forced a decision to be taken to wind up the B.R.M. Trust, I was all the more determined to try to make a success of the venture and the car.

Having found a solution for most of our technical problems in 1953, we entered all the worthwhile races we could, and proved that the car was both fast and dependable and equal to any car put on the road by any of our competitors.

With the new Formula, it is now our determination to produce a successor from the same stable to meet, on behalf of Britain, the world challenge for supremacy. With time now on our side, I have faith that we shall succeed, whilst racing the old B.R.M. cars as long as we can in Formula Libre events.

A.G.B. Owen

David Brown

David Brown also wrote a piece for the book and I was thrilled when he told me that he had had my painting of a DB3S Aston Martin framed and hung on the wall of his office.

He wrote on Monday, 13th September 1954:

> *I came on to the B.R.M. Committee very late in its history, although of course, I was aware of its development from the very beginning. The re-organisation which eventually resulted in it being taken over by Alfred Owen was, I think, a very desirable and necessary thing.*
>
> *Like most advanced technical projects the car took longer to complete than was antici-pated, the result being that it was by no means developed to fruition by the time the new formula came into operation, thus precluding it from Grand Prix racing.*
>
> *Of the possibilities of the design, given time and resources for full development, there can be no doubt, although on some circuits the advantages of a simpler machine must, I think, prevail. No doubt the B.R.M. technicians have acquired a great deal of experience, which I hope will show to full advantage in the new project sponsored by the Owen Organisation.*

Raymond Mays

I continued to correspond with Raymond Mays over the years that followed and he kept me informed about the entirely new 4 cylinder 2.5-litre B.R.M. which was designed for the new Formula.

He wrote to me in April 1953 after I had been unable to meet him in the Paddock at Good-wood because of my father's insistence that we should leave early to avoid the traffic!

> *"Thank you very much for your letter and for your good wishes. I am sorry that you were not able to speak to me at Goodwood, but perhaps better luck another time.*
>
> *Ken Wharton drove a magnifi-cent race and gave us a splendid start to the season, I hope we shall be able to keep it up this year. We are now working very hard for Albi, and we have promised one car, with Ken Wharton driving, for Charterhall on May 23rd. At Albi we hope to have either Fangio or Gonzales but our plans are not quite settled as yet.*
>
> *We are also hoping that there will be a race for which the B.R.M. cars are eligible at Silverstone in July, and we also hope to run at the August Charterhall, and Sept-ember Goodwood. I wish that we could have the race against the Ferraris as you suggest, but it seems that there is no hope of any Grand Prix, other than Albi, this year for which we can enter.*
>
> *We are going ahead with the engine for the new Formula, but I cannot give you any really definite news of our plans yet.*
>
> *Your B.R.M. books will be of the greatest interest in the future, I think you must have one of the most complete records there is."*

A letter from Raymond Mays before the Easter Monday Goodwood meeting in 1953.

The new car, when it arrived, began life rather more dramatically than its predecessor.

In its first race at Oulton Park in September 1955 it appeared at the back of the starting grid, having arrived too late for practice, to be driven by Peter Collins. In the course of the first lap Collins stormed through the field to run fifth. By the tenth lap he was third with only the Maser-

Charles Faroux flags the
B.R.M. of Fangio as he wins
the first heat of the Albi Grand
Prix in May 1953.

Ken Wharton's B.R.M. being
hard pressed by Roy
Salvadori's 250F Maserati, at
Goodwood, on Easter Monday
1954.

atis of Moss and Musso in front of him. Then Collins came into the pits to retire with what he
believed to be falling oil pressure but which turned out to be no more than a faulty gauge!

Unfulfilled promise

After this there was a series of splendid starts by Mike Hawthorn and Tony Brooks followed by
retirements. Worse still, the cars appeared to be lethal. At the Easter Goodwood Meeting in 1956
Mike Hawthorn led at the start and was running second nine laps from the end of the Glover
Trophy when a suspension joint seized causing the car to crash and overturn at top speed at Ford-
water. During the British Grand Prix at Silverstone the throttle linkage failed on Brooks' B.R.M.
so that it rolled over and caught fire. Brooks said afterwards that catching fire and destroying itself
was the only decent thing left for it to do! Mercifully neither driver was seriously injured.

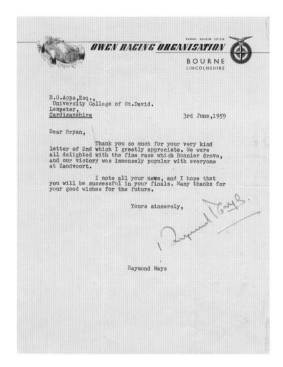

Letter from Raymond Mays in 1959.

Not surprisingly Hawthorn and Brooks left B.R.M. after this and I watched Jean Behra drive a B.R.M. at Goodwood in 1958. Unfortunately his race was all too brief because, as he entered the chicane at high speed right in front of me, his brakes failed and he crashed heavily into the brick wall, destroying the near side corner of the car but, mercifully, not sustaining serious injury to himself.

It was not until 1959 that Joakim Bonnier won the car's first major Grand Prix at Zandvoort. Raymond Mays wrote to me on 3rd June 1959, *"We were all delighted with the fine race which Bonnier drove, and our victory was immensely popular with everyone at Zandvoort."*

Then at the beginning of 1962 Raymond Mays wrote with what turned out to be justified optimism about the 1.5-litre supercharged car designed for what was then the new Formula.

The new V 8 B.R.M. promises well, and the engine gives great hopes for a good showing this year. We expect to run two cars, with Graham Hill and Richie Ginther as our team drivers. We shall probably appear at Snetterton on 14th April, and Goodwood at Easter, before the full Grand Prix season starts on May 20th at Zandvoort.

Tony Rudd

1962 was the year that Graham Hill won the drivers' World Championship after a battle with Jim Clark's Lotus that went on all season. B.R.M. also the Manufacturers World Championship.

Graham Hill in the rear-engined 2.5-litre B.R.M. P48 during the Belgian Grand Prix in 1960.

Tony Rudd wrote to me at the time when Volume Three of Doug Nye's book came out, *"1962 was rather a blur, very exciting. Although he had access to Rubery Owen's records Doug chose not to reproduce the budgets. These showed that we built our own engines and gearboxes as well as the cars, paid the drivers and won the championship for £96,000."*

A visit to Bourne

Kath and I were married on Easter Monday in 1962 and the next year we called at Eastgate House in Bourne to meet Raymond Mays at last. He warmly welcomed us and spoke of his years with the E.R.A.s before the war and with B.R.M. since. He took us to a room containing a gigantic

glass-fronted cabinet that reached from the floor to the ceiling and contained the many trophies he had won over the years. There were the most beautiful silver cups of truly impressive proportions which were quite unlike the monstrosities that are awarded as trophies to winners today. One particularly fine cup, which Prince Bira had also spotted when he called at Eastgate House in 1937, had been won at the Nurburgring in 1935. Afterwards we were taken to the B.R.M.

Graham Hill in his World-Championship-winning B.R.M. at Monaco in 1962.

Jackie Stewart on his way to second place in the Belgian Grand Prix in 1965.

factory which stood in the same grounds and saw a wide range of B.R.Ms including the original V16 car, the 2.5-litre unsupercharged model and the more recent rear-engined contenders.

In 1975 Raymond Mays wrote to me about the changed circumstances of B.R.M. He was beginning to become disillusioned with Formula One and wrote:

> *"Sir Alfred Owen has been too ill to take any active part in B.R.M. for some years, and the firm has been under the direction of Mr and Mrs Louis Stanley. However, this autumn Rubery Owen felt obliged to draw out, and B.R.M. went into voluntary liquidation. It has now been reformed under the name of Stanley B.R.M., and is continuing on a reduced scale in the same premises here. With the reorganisation I felt that I did not any longer want to take any active part, and therefore I resigned my directorship. At the same time my own family businesses were sold, so I have had to get used to a very different way of living. However I am gradually settling down, and I hope to be able to attend a few races this coming season.*
>
> *The prospects for Formula 1 racing do not look too good, as the costs are so enormous, both for running the cars and for organising the race meetings. How well B.R.M. will do now is impossible to say. They are competing with one car in the Argentine G.P on 12th January. You are right; there has never been a car to equal the V-16 if only there had been time to have developed reliability before the change of Formula.*
>
> *I hope things are going well with you, and may I now send my best wishes to you and your wife for 1975.*

We called on Raymond Mays again on August 17th that year with our children Richard and Wendy. He was as charming and courteous as ever and asked Richard and Wendy about their interests and their schools. He told me that the B.R.M. works next door was only a shadow of what it had once been and he would have liked to have seen the old B.R.M. roundel removed from it.

He passed away the following year, a few days after Louis Stanley had managed to supply him, at his request, with some of his favourite tins of watercress soup from Fortnum & Mason.

Graham Hill

Graham Hill was tragically killed when his helicopter crashed in fog. He was a tremendously popular ambassador for the Sport and did a great deal by his own personality to raise the profile of motor racing in this country.

Sir Alfred Owen with the Mark 2 V16 B.R.M. and the 2.5-litre P25 car.

Bette Hill wrote to me of Monaco where she said B.R.M. was really put on the map. She added that every win that Graham had was exciting and he would sit on a pile of old tyres at Monaco

The P25 with high sides. With, from right to left: Rivers Fletcher, Peter Berthon, Raymond Mays and Tony Rudd.

signing autographs for fans and be the very last driver – champion or not – to leave the circuit while she, nanny and the children, waited for him scrunched up in the van. She said *"For him the fans came first!!"*

Louis Stanley wrote of Graham Hill that he was the sport's finest ambassador and was without any hint of arrogance.

Jean and Louis Stanley

Sir Alfred Owen's brother-in-law Louis Stanley and sister Jean who took over B.R.M, had taken a keen interest in the cars from the beginning. Louis Stanley phoned me after I had sent him a painting of Graham Hill at Monaco and said how pleased he was that an Anglican vicar should take such an interest in motor racing, and joked that most of the clergy in his diocese looked as though could hardly complete a lap of the cathedral! When Kath and I called on the Stanleys one afternoon at Trumpington I saw that my painting had been propped up against the cup that had been won at Monaco. We were shown a vast album of photographs the Stanleys had taken at

Kath and I, with Louis and Jean Stanley, at their home in Trumptington.

motor races and elsewhere over the years. They both signed my scrapbook and Louis wrote in it, *"A unique record compiled by a genuine enthusiast."*

In 2001 Louis Stanley invited Kath and I to the launch of his book *Vignettes and Memories* at the Dorchester in London. Jean had been taken ill and was unable to be there and I later sent a further B.R.M. painting which he told me he had placed by the side of her bed where she could see it.

He was heartbroken when Jean died, and I had long conversations with him by phone in the months that followed. He told me that he had established himself as a publisher purely of his own books and one based on my B.R.M. Scrapbooks. Sadly he did not live to see that.

MOTOR RACING AFTER THE WAR

MOTOR RACING could not be reinstated either at Brooklands or at Donington Park after the War because of the destructive effects of their occupation by the military, so it was decided to use the perimeter roads of the war timeairfields of Silverstone in Northamptonshire and Westhampnett in Sussex instead.

Goodwood

The use of Westhampnett on the Goodwood estate was the idea of Squadron Leader Tony Gaze. Being a racing driver, Gaze discussed it with the Duke of Richmond and Gordon, who had raced at Brooklands before the war as Freddie March, and who offered his enthusiastic support. The race meetings at Silverstone were organised by the British Racing Drivers' Club and at Goodwood by the British Automobile Racing Club, and the first Goodwood meeting was held on September 18 1948. The circuit consisted of 2.4 miles of resurfaced road with a concrete barrier and chestnut fencing to separate it from the spectators. Eighty-five drivers competed in the day's programme watched by a crowd of 15,000. There was a rudimentary paddock but no pits, no grandstands and grossly inadequate crowd control, but it was a great success. The main event was won by Reg Parnell in a 4CLT "San Remo" Maserati and Stirling Moss won the event for 500cc cars. What might be called the "Spirit of Goodwood" was born.

Easter Monday Meeting 1949

Through being taken to the next big meeting at Goodwood by my parents at the age of twelve, I caught the "motor racing bug". I still have the race programme, now much worn, with Reg Parnell's Maserati on the cover. Some grandstands and other essential facilities were provided, but there was still a long way to go. Six five-lap races took place, three of them being handicaps, and a ten-lap race for the Richmond Trophy. The fuel used by the cars contained a high percentage of methanol and they emitted a strong sweet smell which pervaded the circuit. Crash helmets were recommended but not compulsory, and all the competitors had to complete a parade lap before the start and a further slow lap at the end of the race. They had to ballot for their places in the starting grid and the Richmond Trophy Race was broadcast by the B.B.C. We spent most of the day at Madgwick Corner where the cars could be seen streaming away from the start. John Heath drove an H.W. Alta, Reg Parnell and Ashmore the two Scuderia Ambrosiana-entered 4CLT Maseratis, Denis Poore a pre-war 3.8-litre Alfa Romeo, Kenneth McAlpine a 1930s 2.9-litre Maserati and there were five E.R.A.s. Reg Parnell won both the Chichester Cup and the Richmond Trophy.

At the Easter Monday meeting in 1950 Parnell again won the main event but Baron de Graffenried and Prince Bira challenged him with their similar cars and in the end Brian Shaw-Taylor finished third behind Parnell and de Graffenried.

The following September Reg Parnell won the two main events but this time in the new V16 B.R.M. It was hailed as a great triumph, but it subsequently became apparent that these short races, run in appallingly wet conditions, were not true tests of the car's speed or reliability.

The British Grand Prix at Silverstone

The first British Grand Prix was held at Silverstone in 1949 and it was won by Baron de Graffenreid's Maserati from Bob Gerard's E.R.A. The next year it was became a World Championship event and the 158 Alfa Romeos of Guiseppe Farina, Luigi Fagioli and Reg Parnell took the first three places. There were two of the fabulous 4.5-litre unsupercharged Lago Talbots also running and the E.R.A.s of Bob Gerard and Cuth Harrison. In *The British Racing Hero* by Derick Allsop, Reg Parnell's son Tim recalled, *"After the British Grand Prix at Silverstone there was a celebration at Alfa's hotel in Northampton. Members of the team had dinner together, then gathered round a piano for a sing-song. It was a friendly atmosphere. Sport and comradeship were what mattered. Motor racing is a million miles from that today."*

Baron de Graffenried winning the British Grand Prix at Silverstone in his 4CLT Maserati in 1949.

Bob Gerard coming second in the British Grand Prix in 1949.

The start of the Richmond Trophy race at Goodwood in 1951, with Parnell's Maserati slightly ahead of Bira's O.S.C.A.

Later Goodwood events

A major part source of interest and enjoyment in motor racing after the war was the sheer spectacle of those fine old cars with their "have a go" drivers. In 1951 Prince Bira came to Goodwood with his 4.5-litre O.S.C.A. which had been built by the Maserati brothers, after Count Orsini had taken over Maserati, using a modified 4CLT chassis. The car looking impressive with its large vertically slatted oval grill and its blue and yellow livery and went well. All the cars in those days

Painting of Juan Fangio coming second at Silverstone in the British Grand Prix in 1951, signed by Fangio.

appeared to be enormous because their drivers wore leather helmets or hard hats of similar size instead of the vast helmets which the drivers are compelled to wear today. Of course it's good that drivers are far better protected today, but it remains the case that a space-helmeted driver in a 158 Alfa Romeo or an E.R.A. dwarfs the car and, to my mind, makes it look slightly ridiculous.

Hawthorn's Cooper Bristol

In 1952 Mike Hawthorn and the Cooper Bristols made their debut. I was hoping that George Abecassis would win in his lone H.W.M. as the team had been the first to uphold the flag for Britain consistently abroad and so I was delighted to see the H.W.M. at the front of the pack as the cars approached the last bend of the first lap. But Abecassis went straight off the course in the middle of the bend without reducing speed, while Hawthorn went on to win in his new and unpainted Cooper Bristol! When he drove round his victory lap he removed his helmet to reveal a shock of blond hair which made quite an impression on the young and perhaps not so young ladies in the crowd! Eric Brandon and Alan Brown drove the works' Cooper Bristols and Juan Fangio was given a fourth car, which was slow because it had constantly been used to test the design during its development.

Many years later, when I sent George Abeccasis a painting of him at a later race at Silverstone, I recalled the incident at Goodwood.

He wrote:

> *"I thank you most sincerely for your gift of the painting of the H.W.M.*
>
> *I well remember that day at Goodwood: we had re-piped the brakes in steel pipes instead of copper and had neglected to clip the cross pipe at the front of the chassis – it broke with vibration when I was hoping to win!*
>
> *I remember too the day which is the subject of your painting – the differential seized and the car became too non competitive.*
>
> *If only we had had a really good engine we might have done something more worthwhile."*

I see the B.R.Ms at last!

Stirling Moss was featured on the cover of the Goodwood programme for Easter 1953 which provided me with my first opportunity to see the B.R.M.s in action. Raymond Mays had sent me a letter which would have enabled me to meet him in the paddock at the end of the day but, sadly, my father insisted on leaving early to avoid the traffic and in 1953 parents tended to be obeyed by their teenage sons! In spite of that it was a memorable day. I heard the V16 B.R.M. engines being started up in the paddock from a quarter of a mile away and, when they were racing, I could hear them as they drove all around the course, above the sound of the cars that were actually passing the point where I stood! Reg Parnell and Ken Wharton drove the two B.R.M.s and Piero Taruffi the 4.5-litre "Thinwall Special" Ferrari. Baron de Graffenried was in his 1952 2-litre unsupercharged Maserati A6GCM and there were also Formula 2 Cooper Bristols, Connaughts and Stirling Moss' Cooper Alta. It rained for the Chichester Cup which meant that De Graffenreid had more grip on the road than the larger cars. The B.R.Ms suffered from wheel

Reg Parnell's B.R.M. through the lens of my Brownie box camera at Goodwood in 1953.

spin, unable to put their superior power down on to the track, and the result was that de Graffenried won the race from Wharton's B.R.M. with Parnell finishing fourth. In drier conditions Ken Wharton led away from the start of the Richmond Trophy Race and set a new lap record of 92.91mph. Baron de Graffenried held on to second place until he was overtaken by Pierro Taruffi in the "Thinwall Special". In the handicap races for sports car race the C- Type Jaguars took on J2 Allards, Healey Silverstones, XK20 Jaguars and Aston Martin DB2s.

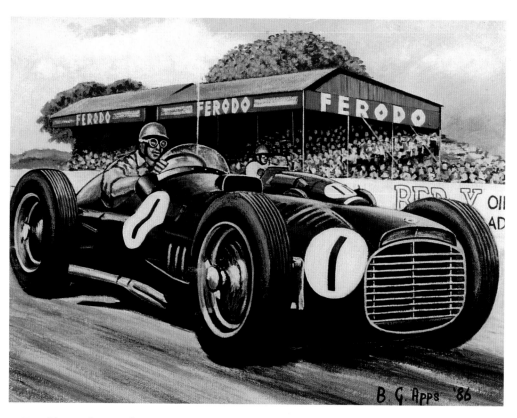

In addition during the 1950s there were the annual Goodwood Nine Hours Races which enabled the spectators to see the cars racing with their headlights piercing the darkness of night. I could never persuade my father to go to the "Nine Hours" but, in fairness to him, it would have meant starting out from Bishopstoke after he had come home from his business when the race was already well underway. It was argued that Goodwood was too small a circuit for a long distance race because the slower cars were lapped so frequently and it was said that many spectators lost interest and went back to their homes after dark. But it did bring something of the flavour of Le Mans to this country and must have been of absorbing interest to genuine enthusiasts. Unlike Le Mans during that period, the Goodwood distance races seemed to favour John Wyer's Aston Martin team rather than Lofty England's Jaguars. John Wyer and Raymond "Lofty" England were both great team managers. Wyer had a number of outstanding successes at Le Mans with Ford GT40s and Porsches between 1966 and 1975. He told me that my painting of the Goodwood Nine Hours Race *"combined the unique contrast between the placid beauty of the Sussex countryside and the noise and tension of motor racing."* Lofty England had helped develop Tim Birkin's "Blower" Bentleys before the war, and worked at E.R.A. until he unwisely suggested that Raymond Mays had been too heavy on the brakes! He became a Joint Managing Director of Jaguar cars in 1967.

Tony Rolt drove a number of cars at Goodwood, including Rob Walker's pre war ex Richard Seaman Delage fitted with an E-Type E.R.A. engine, and Jaguars in the Nine Hours' Races. He wrote to me *"I am not surprised that you were "bitten" at the early age of 12."* Major A.P.R. Rolt was captured at Boulogne before the evacuation of Dunkirk. He was imprisoned in Colditz Castle and became involved in the attempt to escape from Colditz in a glider. He and Duncan Hamilton led the Nine Hours Races at Goodwood more than once but something always seemed to go wrong.

One of the great Italian drivers who emerged immediately after the war driving a 4CLT Maserati was Luigi Villoresi. He wrote to me about his professional career.

> *"Thank you very much indeed for your beautiful water colour. It is an absolutely perfect portrait of me in the 12 cylinder Ferrari 4500 with which I took part in – and won – the 1952 "Daily Mail Trophy" this however was not held at Silverstone but, if I am not mistaken, on the Goodwood track.*
>
> *This racing car was a unique development, and remained the only 4500 type; it had already entered various races winning several with Ascari, myself and Gonzales.*

Gonzales' race at Silverstone put an end to the supremacy of the famous twin-compressor Alfetta 1500: this was in 1951.

"My life as a professional racing driver began in 1937 with Maserati. In their cars I won over twenty-five races, winning the Italian Championship in 1937 for the class up to 1500 cc, and two Italian absolute Championships in 1939 and 1947.

In 1949 I went over to Ferrari, and in their cars I won twenty-two races, among these were the 1951 Mille Miglia, the 1952 Tour of Sicily and, with Ascari, I was second absolute at the Carrera Mexicana.

In 1954 I moved on to Lancia with Ascari, and in the sports car I won the Oporto Race and the Tour of Tuscany.

I was also very fond of rallies. In my spare time I won the Monte Carlo Rally in a Fiat for the up to 1500 cc class, as well as the Sestriere Rally and the very trying Acropolis Rally in a Lancia B20.

I waved goodbye to my life as a sportsman in 1955."

Once more I'd like to thank you for the superb souvenir you sent me, which is very dear to me"

I never saw the 158 Alfa Romeos in action but was gratified when the great Juan Fangio told me that my paintings of him in the Alfa and the W196 Mercedes would be exhibited in the Motor Museum bearing his name which was to be opened in his native town of Balcarce on November 22nd. 1986.

Racing Cars in the 1950s

The 1950s saw the rapid development in racing cars in Italy, Germany and Great Britain while France was well represented early on with their beautiful Lago Talbots and little Gordinis. In 1956 a brand new Bugatti appeared at Rheims for the French Grand Prix. It was designed by Columbo and had a box-section space frame. The straight 8 cylinder engine was mounted transversely behind the driver, and it even had the shape of the traditional Bugatti radiator represented at the front. It was driven by Maurice Trintignant but retired on lap 18. Under-funded, it was not seen again. On the other hand Maseratis made great strides from the 4CLT to the 2-litre A6GCM of 1952 and then to the A6SSG in 1953. The next year the famous 250F car appeared and it was progressively developed in the years that followed. Ferrari began the 1950s with their V12 4.5-litre car and this was followed by the all-conquering four cylinder Ferrari 500 in 1952. The 2.5 litre Tipo 555 Super Squalo cars were introduced to compete, though unsuccessfully, with the W196 Mercedes Benz in their streamlined and unstreamlined forms. Then came the fabulous Lancia D50s which were handed over to Enzo Ferrari, and from which the Lancia Ferraris were developed, and after that the Ferrari Dino 246. From Great Britain the P25 B.R.M. created great drama in the hands of Mike Hawthorn and Tony Brooks, and a succession of Vanwalls appeared, beginning with a car that wore its radiator strangely on top of its bonnet, and ending with the Frank Costin designed wind cheating winners. Then there were Coopers, Lotuses including the front engined Lotus 16, and of course Connaughts. There was certainly plenty to arrest the eye in the 1950s and no suggestion of the uniformity which characterises the modern starting grid.

(Left) Signed photograph of Baron de Graffenried in his A6SSG Maserati.

(Right) Signed painting of Fangio, winning the 1957 German Grand Prix, to gain his fifth World Championship title after an epic race.

JOHN COOPER AND THE MID-ENGINED REVOLUTION

I N HIS foreword to John Cooper's autobiography Ken Tyrrell wrote, *"John really enjoyed motor racing and, when he was having a good time, so was everyone else."*

Louis Stanley, in *Behind the Scenes,* expressed a similar view with typical style and finesse. *"Without him the prairie oyster would have lost its Worcester sauce and roast beef its horse radish. Certainly motor racing would have been the poorer without the personality of John Cooper."*

From this it will be obvious that John Cooper was an extremely likeable character and, even though he had such a profound influence on the design of racing cars since the war, he was always modest and unassuming.

In 1932, when John was nine years old, his father Charles built him a racing car, scaled down to his proportions, and powered by a lawn mower engine. This was followed when he was eleven by a sports car with an Austin Seven engine. Both cars were beautifully made and John must have been the envy of all his friends.

His quiet revolution which was to redraw the basic rules of racing car design on both sides of the Atlantic began in the modest Cooper Garage in Surbiton where, in the late 1940s he and his father Charles decided to build inexpensive racing cars from materials that were cheap to acquire and readily available. Simplicity of design was their guiding principle.

John Cooper with the JAP-engined Cooper 500.

It is true that Auto Union built mid-engined racing cars which were famous in the 1930s but, even with the help of Bernd Rosemeyer and Tazio Nuvolari, they failed to establish a clear superiority over their front-engined rivals. One could say that the jury was still out after the war and, when cars with their engines mounted between the drivers and the rear wheels, started to become more numerous on the starting grids I wrote to the *Motoring News* asking whether this just a passing fashion or was it here to stay? The editor declined to comment and merely invited his readers to make their own judgement on the issue!

The Cooper 500

The Cooper 500 was powered by a single cylinder JAP or Norton motorcycle engine which was situated where it could deliver its power most directly by means of a simple chain to the rear wheels. The cars were built from welding together the front halves of two old Fiat Topolino cars and only when the Coopers began to run out of second hand Fiats did they manufacture their chasses from scratch. The Cooper was sold for £500, had a top speed of 108mph, and went from naught to sixty in eight seconds.

The prototype was driven by John Cooper in the Prescott Hillclimb in 1946 and Stirling Moss was amongst the first to buy a Cooper 500 when they went on sale in 1948. He won his first race with it at Goodwood in September that year. Moss wrote in *Stirling Moss My Cars, My Career* that the revs had to be kept at near maximum at all times to sustain the car's power. The Cooper 500, while being entirely unpretentious, was a fine looking car even though John and Charles would not have agonised over its aesthetics. In 1950 a Mark 2 version appeared which, as well as saving vital ounces, was even more pleasing to the eye.

A race for 500cc cars became an essential ingredient at every major motor race meeting, supporting the main event, and it was always popular with the crowds because it assured them of good entertainment. The less skilful drivers would pirouette in the centre of the track while others nipped past on either side. The cars were immensely stable and seldom turned over, no matter with how much abandon they were thrown about. At the same time the cream inevitably rose to the top and Stirling Moss, with his car complete with horseshoe and No 7, became the one to beat. Bernie Ecclestone drove a Cooper 500 as did Ken Tyrrell, who described to me years later how he once had the distinction of overtaking Stirling Moss on a bend. The problem was, he explained, that only Stirling emerged from the bend as the speed of his own car was too great for him to control! Stirling Moss also drove a 500cc Keift which became a rival to the Coopers.

Don Parker

One of the most successful entrants in 500cc, or Formula Three races as they came to be known, was Don Parker who drove the JAP engined CTS or Charlie Smith Special. Charlie Smith was killed while practising for a motorcycle race in 1948 and his widow gave the car to Don. He weighed less than eight stone and went to extreme lengths to save as much additional weight as possible, even driving without his underwear! He also bought and modified a Keift and won three Formula Three Championships by the age of fifty.

Don Parker in his C.F.S. car at Goodwood in 1949.

My painting of Don was taken by his wife Dora to Chichester Hospital where he was recovering from an eye operation. Unrecognised before, she told me that it instantly made him a celebrity, with all the doctors and nurses wanting to stand and chat to him about his experiences behind the wheel. He later sent me a post card from Antigua where he was recuperating.

The Cooper Bristol

The Formula Two 2-litre Cooper Bristol, which appeared at Goodwood in 1952, had its engine placed conventionally in the front as it had not yet dawned upon John or his father Charles that,

Mike Hawthorn finishing third in the Cooper-Bristol, at the British Grand Prix in 1952.

with the Cooper 500's layout, they had really stumbled upon a winning design. Four Cooper Bristols were initially built for Eric Brandon, Alan Brown and Mike Hawthorn, the fourth being driven by Juan Fangio at the Easter Monday race meeting. The engine was essentially the BMW 328 which had been taken over by the Bristol Aeroplane Company after the war. It could hold its own against the Alta engined H.W.M.s and the Lea Frances-engined Connaughts and these front-engined Coopers were sold for just £2000. Mike Hawthorn shot to stardom that Easter Monday at Goodwood driving his as yet unpainted car ahead of all the others. It later emerged that the large air scoop on top of the bonnet of his car was designed to intimidate the opposition rather than to hide any mechanical secrets, and that his impressive speed was in part due to the use of a higher octane fuel than the rest. That is not to detract from the outstanding ability of Mike Hawthorn who finished in third place with his Cooper Bristol in the British Grand Prix at Silverstone later that year behind the Ferraris of Alberto Ascari and Piero Taruffi.

A Mark 2 Cooper Bristol appeared in 1953 with a lighter tubular frame and a modified radiator which meant that even the standard air scoop could be eliminated.

A Cooper-Alta Special was built for Stirling Moss in 1953 by Ray Martin, Alf Francis and Tony Robinson, around a car that began its life as a Cooper, but the project was beset with problems and the car proved to be unsatisfactory. Then a second Cooper-Alta Special was built by Alf Francis and Tony Robinson and this time they used a standard Formula 2 Cooper chassis. The car used nitro-methane fuel and had a lot more power than its predecessor and Stirling, who wanted to drive a British car if possible, had successes with it both at Crystal Palace and at Prescott. At the same time it forced him to the conclusion that it was necessity to drive a foreign car to compete on even terms with the very best.

Alan Brown

Alan Brown with Eric Brandon drove the Ecurie Richmond Cooper Bristols. He was known as "Chiron" Brown because, like the French driver, his pale blue helmet and overalls were always immaculate. He had been an Army major during the war and afterwards sold a motor mower to

Signed photograph of Alan Brown in a D-Type Jaguar, with little protection for the crowd.

the Royal Family just to gain the privilege of using the Royal Coat of Arms and the words "By Appointment"! In addition to Coopers he raced D-Type Jaguars and sent me a photograph of himself driving an Ecurie Ecosse D-Type at Goodwood. He wrote, *"Motor racing is so very different now, very boring."*

Return to Mid-Engined Cars

In 1955 John Cooper produced stub-tailed mid-engined sports cars with twin cam engines that were developed from the Coventry-Climax fire pump engine, and a single seater version which was intended for Formula Two events. It was at this point that he came to see the clear advantages of placing the engine behind the driver. David Tremayne recorded in *Grandprix.com* that John

Jack Brabham winning the Monaco Grand Prix in his Cooper-Climax in 1959.

Jack Brabham winning the World Championship in the Copper-Climax in 1960.

Cooper said the sports car *"really was a super little car, light, easy on its tyres, well balanced. And cheap. It just seemed so right."*

Stirling Moss proved the advantages of Cooper's design when he won the 1958 Argentine Grand Prix in Rob Walker's dark blue 2.2-litre Coventry-Climax engined Cooper, beating the front-engined Ferraris of Luigi Musso and Mike Hawthorn and no less than six 250F Maseratis led by Fangio, all of which had 2.5-litre engines. It has to be admitted that much of this was due to the superlative skill of Moss who managed to nurse his threadbare tyres to complete the race without a pit stop. Nevertheless the superiority of the Cooper's layout was clear for all to see and although Colin Chapman produced his Lotus 16 with a front-mounted Coventry-Climax engine in 1958 he adopted Cooper's arrangement for his later cars. The amazingly successful partnership of Colin Chapman, Jim Clark and the light but fragile Lotus cars is of course another story.

John Cooper introduced another important innovation in 1958 and this was threaded joints in the rear suspension of the cars, enabling them to be adjusted according to circumstances. It was the beginning of a trend that was to lead to the infinitely adjustable racing cars of the future.

In 1959 and 1960 Jack Brabham won the World Championship driving a Grand Prix Cooper with a Coventry-Climax engine enlarged to a full 2.5-litres. In 1959 Cooper-Climax won the Constructors' World Championship and Cooper-Climax drivers came first, third, sixth, seventh and tenth in the Drivers' World Championship, an astonishing result that was nevertheless exceeded the following year.

Innes Ireland

This was a time when small setups were sometimes able to beat the big boys. Innes Ireland wrote to me about how he beat Bonnier's Porsche in the Solitude Grand Prix in 1961 on Porsche's own ground with the B.R.P.

> *"The origin of the BRP car was simply that Ken Gregory decided to manufacture their own cars and no doubt you remember the initials stood for British Racing Partnership. The BRP car was a monocoque designed by Tony Robinson who was the Team's Chief Mechanic. It was based on the Lotus 25 but unhappily did not handle nearly as well and in reality was not a great success. Tony was an excellent engineer, the car was beautifully built but with Tony not being a true racing car designer the suspension never worked as well as that on the Lotus 25."*

John Cooper was also famous for his Mini Coopers which on the race track provided a level of entertainment that rivalled that of the 500cc racing cars.

Innes Ireland winning the Solitude Grand Prix in 1961.

High Jinks

Ken Tyrrell wrote in John Cooper's autobiography that in the late fifties there seemed to be more fun and more characters like John. He recalled the occasion when the American driver Masten Gregory drew into the pits during a Formula Two race at Rheims after only four laps complaining of the heat. John had a bucket full of cold water thrown into his cockpit and told him to get back into the race saying to others, *"It cost me £20,000 to build that car for him and he tells me he's hot."* Cooper described in his book the high jinks that the drivers got up to in his day. He related how when they were at Bel Air for the Riverside Grand Prix in 1960 Walt Hansgen, who drove a D-Type Jaguar for Briggs Cunningham, accepted a bet that he would act upon an advertisement of Avis that said, *"Pick up your rented car and leave it wherever you like."* He parked his car in the swimming pool of the local motel and watched it sink to the bottom, remembering just in time to retrieve his camera from the back! The incident is strikingly similar that which Professor Sid Watkins ascribed to Innes Ireland and I will leave it to the reader to make a judgement as to their veracity.

Swimming pools seemed to fascinate the drivers and in 1948 some of them, having driven their competition cars along the Madeira Drive to the Majestic Hotel for the Jersey International Road Race, poured petrol and benzol into the swimming pool and set it alight. It was indeed a very different era.

Harry Schell

The first United States Grand Prix was held at Sebring in 1959 and, amazingly, on the front row of the starting grid alongside the 2.5-litre Cooper-Climaxs of Stirling Moss and Jack Brabham was the 2.2-litre car of Harry Schell.

The story is told in detail by John Cooper with John Bentley in *John Cooper Grand Prix Carpet-Bagger.*

"Before closing the story of the first U.S. Grand Prix at Sebring, there is a story I must tell even though it means backtracking a little. It concerns the qualifications and starting grid positions and how the late Harry Schell threw a monkey wrench in the works that really caused something of a panic. That it was meant as a practical joke did nothing to mitigate against the wrath it provoked.

Schell's 2.2 litre Climax-powered Cooper was one of several private entries bearing our factory name but not connected with the Surbiton works. In the final grid, the front row was occupied by Moss (Cooper-Climax), Jack Brabham, and Tony Brooks in a Ferrari. But suddenly, overnight, Schell was moved up into the front row along with Moss and Brabham, while poor Brooks was relegated to the second row. No one appeared to have noticed Schell's "fastest time" and the whole thing came as a bombshell which really angered Tavoni, the Ferrari team manager. Until that drastic last-minute change, the best time anyone had on Schell had been 3: 11: 2. There was no possible way he could have returned a time between 3: 3 (Jack's fastest lap) and 3: 5: 8 (Tony's best), Leaving aside the driving, Schell's car just did not have enough steam and not even Fangio could have clocked the time he claimed, yet apparently there it was on the lap score charts, plain for everyone to see. If Tavoni was mad, so was Rob Walker, two of whose independent Cooper entries, driven by Moss and Trintignant, also were in the race. But Schell screamed loud and clear and his claim stood and there he was, in the front row, when the starting flag dropped.

Now as to what actually happened Schell, who was given to practical jokes in a big way, thought it would be hysterically funny if he could fool the official timers. And he did, by a very simple trick which no one observed, but which he freely admitted later.

At Sebring, just beyond the MG Bridge and before entering the Esses, there is a sharp turn off the course that seemingly led nowhere. Certainly it was not part of the circuit, but Schell found out that it connected with the right-left elbow at the end of the Warehouse Straight, bypassing the entire straight and the Warehouse Hairpin with its tricky sand pile. So he quietly cut across, motoring back onto the course during a momentary lull in the traffic – and cut about seven seconds off his lap time!

It seems from what is recorded later in the book that Harry Schell got his comeuppance, and it occurred before the French Grand Prix at Rheims in 1959 where Schell was to drive a B.R.M.

> *"Schell arrived in a small German mini-car called the Goggomobile. This pint-sized machine apparently was too much of a temptation for some of the boys and this time Harry was on the receiving end of a practical joke. During one of the evenings after practice, Schell went out with the most beautiful bird, leaving his car outside the hotel. While he was enjoying dinner in one of the many good restaurants nearby, the boys seized their chance. They bodily carried the tiny, lightweight Goggomobile into the hotel and up the stairs and dumped it outside Harry's bedroom door. What was even worse, they placed it so that he couldn't even open the door to get into his room when he returned. It was a long time before he was able to get the car down and back on the road again, and meantime he was denied the use of his bedroom and even a change of clothes!"*

The Cooper-Maserati

In 1966 the T81 Cooper-Maserati appeared for the new 3-litre Formula. It had a full monocoque body and a V12 Maserati engine. In addition to the works team, Cooper-Maseratis were bought by Rob Walker, Joakim Bonnier and Guy Ligier. John Surtees won the Mexican Grand Prix in a works Cooper-Maserati at the end of the 1966 season and Joakim Rindt finished third that year in the World Champion driving for Cooper. Pedro Rodrigues won the South African Grand Prix in a Cooper-Maserati in 1967. The following year John Cooper adopted the V12 B.R.M. engine for his cars instead and these cars finished in third and fourth places at Monaco.

The Repco Brabhams

Jack Brabham seized the opportunity of the 3-litre Formula in 1966 to build his Oldsmobile based V8 Repco engined Brabhams. He won the World Championship in 1966 in a Repco Brabham, while Denny Hume and he came first and second in the 1967 World Championship with two of his cars. He wrote to me in 1988 *"Although the Brabham team are not competing this year, all three of my sons are keeping the name alive in motor racing. Geoffrey is doing very well in America and Gary and David are racing in this country. Who knows, one day you may be able to paint another Brabham in another Grand Prix."*

Doug Nye records in *Cooper Cars* that John Cooper and Major Terry Owens ran the Mini-Cooper team with Ginger Devlin through 1969 after which *"the man whose enthusiasm had really started it all with Eric Brandon back in 1946 took a garage at Ferring on the Sussex coast and settled for a more peaceful life in the motor trade."*

Jack Brabham winning the Dutch Grand Prix in his Repco Brabham, in 1966.

SHOWING THE
FLAG ABROAD

H.W.M.

I WAS AS enthusiastic a supporter of H.W.M. in Formula Two as I was of B.R.M. in Formula One because John Heath and George Abecassis were the first British manufacturers in motor racing to show the flag abroad after the war.

George Abecassis drove an Austin Seven at Brooklands in 1935 and later bought an Alta with which he won the Imperial Trophy Race in 1939.

He became a pilot in the R.A.F. at the outbreak of war and was Squadron Leader of the "Moon Squadron" that ferried secret agents to and from occupied France in Lysander aircraft. After being shot down he attempted to escape by taking the controls of a German aircraft but he discovered that "all the controls said auf and zu and bloody stuff like that and we thought 'there are better ways of getting killed!'" He was taken prisoner and was confined in Colditz Castle from which he also attempted to escape. Doug Nye wrote of Abecassis in his obituary "he was great fun, a real effortless character, tough, languid, unconcerned, a drinker, a gentleman."

John Heath with the H.W. Alta in 1949.

John Heath and George Abecassis

Immediately after the war Abecassis teamed up with John Heath to establish Hersham and Walton Motors at Walton-on-Thames and in 1948 they built an HW Alta which was entered for sports car races. John Heath won the Manx Cup in 1949 and came second in the Grand Prix de l'ACF at Comminges.

1950

Encouraged by this measure of success, Heath and Abecassis, with Polish refugee Alf Francis as the Chief Mechanic, built three H.W.M.s in 1950. The cars had two seats and four cylinder 2-litre Alta engines and could be used in sports car races as well as events for outright racing cars in stripped down form. They were equipped with Armstrong Siddeley pre selector gearboxes. Two new H.W.M.s retired in their initial outing in the Lavant Cup race for Formula Two cars at Good-wood in the hands of Heath and Abecassis. Then, as the season continued, the team took on the Ferraris and Simca Gordinis abroad and were a popular British presence in Europe. They raced at Roubaix, Mons and Aix-les-Bains, and the Belgian driver and band leader Johnny Claes gained their first win at Chimay in May. Stirling Moss joined the team and was offered 25 per cent of both starting money and prize money which,

Moss records in Menard and Vassal's *Stirling Moss: The Champion Without a Crown* amounted to some £200 a race. *"After the race we would go to a party to pick up our prize money and we often had a good time."* Stirling Moss said that he learned a great deal about driving a racing car as a member of a team through his time with H.W.M. He drove with his seemingly relaxed style, with his arms stretched out to the steering wheel, to undermine the confidence of his competitors, and later managed to have his own 250F Maserati stretched to accommodate this technique.

Stirling Moss drove an H.W.M. at Monthery and in other races on the Continent and was challenging for third place in a Formula One race at Caracalla when he lost a wheel. He also ran in third place at Rheims and Bari. Lance Macklin was often his team mate and the two finished second and third at Mettet while Moss claimed third place at Perigueux. Although Stirling Moss was ten years younger than Lance Macklin the two were good friends.

Stirling Moss in his H.W.M. at Goodwood in 1951.

1951 and the Single Seater

For 1951 a team of single seater H.W.M.s were built with tubular chasses, and full details with a cut away drawing of the car appeared in *Autosport*. Their front suspension was by double wishbones and coil springs and the rear a de Dion with torsion bars. The 2-litre engine, designed by Geoffrey Taylor, was developed by R.R. Jackson and the cars were slimmer, lighter and faster than the previous models, being designed solely for pure race car events. They looked like the real thing and I poured over photographs of them in the motoring Press and eagerly watched Stirling Moss and Lance Macklin drive them at Goodwood that Easter Monday. After a poor start Moss came through the field to pass Eric Brandon's Cooper during the final lap to win the race. Moss finished in second place at Aix-les-Bains and came third in a Formula One race at Zandvoort. Macklin came second at Angouleme and third at Modena and Harry Schell picked up a third place at Posilippo. Yves Girand-Cabantous joined the team in mid season and became one of its regular drivers. At Marseilles Moss came third behind Villoresi's Ferrari and Trintignant's Gordini. At San Remo the two came fifth and seventh in a field that contained Ferraris and Bira's O.S.C.A. of 4.5-litres. At Genoa Moss led the race from the Ferraris of Ascari and Villoresi and believed that he might have won the race if his differential hadn't failed. The two H.W.M.s were up against the larger Formula One cars at Berne for the Swiss Grand Prix and Moss coped well until his windscreen shattered and the current of air threatened to remove his helmet and goggles! He held seventh place before running out of fuel. Moss was fastest in practice in Aix-les-Bains, won his heat and came second in the Final with a rough engine. Choosing to honour his commitment to drive for H.W.M. Stirling refused an invitation from Enzo Ferrari to drive one of his cars. How very differently things might have worked out for him in subsequent years had he not declined that opportunity! At Avus with H.W.M., the engines of both his and Macklin's cars failed under the stress of speeding on the extremely fast, banked circuit. Macklin notched up a second place at Angouleme and a third at Modena while the irrepressible Harry Schell came second in an H.W.M. at Posilippo. At Goodwood Moss, Abecassis and Hamilton came first, second and third in the Madgwick Cup and, at the end of the year Moss, Abecassis and Duncan Hamilton gained the first three places at Winfield.

1952

Formula Two received World Championship status in 1952 partly because of the withdrawal of the Alfa Romeo from Formula One and partly because it was felt that the V16 B.R.M. could not be relied upon. It has been said that the performance of the Alta engine in the H.W.M.s led to it influencing the design of the all conquering Ferrari 500. Peter Collins joined the H.W.M. team with Lance Macklin and Yves Girand Cabantous and others, including John Heath, Duncan Hamilton, Tony Rolt, Paul Frere and Jack Fairman drove the cars occasionally too.

In all H.W.M. competed in eight races in France, the first being at Pau where split brake pipes put out Collins and Macklin, and Cabantous retired with locking brakes. Abecassis drove an H.W.M. at Goodwood on Easter Monday, as recorded elsewhere, and also retired with brake trouble. The high point of the year was the *Daily Express* International Trophy Race at Silverstone where Macklin and Rolt came first and second. Moss was second at Chimay and Frere won the Grand Prix des Frontieres. In the Eifelrennen on the Nurburgring Moss finished second and Duncan Hamilton took fourth place. Yet in 1952 the Cooper Bristol had been proved to be the faster car.

1953

At the beginning of 1953 H.W.M. was short of funds. The cars' Alta engines had new cylinder heads with gear-driven camshafts in place of the chain driven ones. But they were heavy and outclassed by their competitors. They sported remodelled fronts with open air ducts in place of the chromium slatted grills which did not, in my estimation, enhance their appearance. Duncan Hamilton won the first heat of the Ulster Trophy at Dundrod and came sixth in the Final, but the team's mechanics were overworked in trying to cope with successive problems between races.

1954

Hopes for a new car with a 2.5-litre Alta engine designed for the new Formula in 1954 were not realised, and a V8 Coventry-Climax engine failed to arrive.

H.W.M. concentrated on building and racing Jaguar-engined sports racing cars and, in 1956, John Heath was killed driving one of these in the Mille Miglia. After this George Abecassis turned his attention to running the business.

CONNAUGHT

Rodney Clark of Continental Cars Limited in Send was joined by Kenneth McAlpine, the head of the large construction company, to found Connaught Engineering in 1947. They built a limited number sports racing car using a 1767cc Lea Francis engine, one of which was raced by McAlpine himself.

The Type A Connaught

Next they turned their attention to a single seater racing car for Formula Two, and Mike Oliver was brought in to assist with the production of the A-Type Connaught with its much modified four cylinder twin camshaft Lea Frances engine enlarged to 1964cc. It had torsion bar and wish-

Stirling Moss driving a works A-Type Connaught in the 1952 Italian Grand Prix.

bone four-wheel independent suspension at first but later a de Dion system was adopted. The cars had expensive cast alloy wheels instead of spokes and, like the H.W.M.s, a pre-selector gear box. The Connaughts of Rodney Clark were well engineered and beautifully crafted. The curvaceous tail of the Type A Connaught alone involved a great deal of painstaking work to construct and, more importantly, to rebuild after racing incidents, but it amounted to a work of art. Nine A-Types were built for 1951 and Rob Walker bought one which was often driven by Tony Rolt and at times by Stirling Moss. Writing of his A-Type Connaught, Rob Walker told me, *"As you say, the Connaught driven so well by Tony Rolt was mine and in fact still is in the same colours sitting in the museum at Donington. That car in 1953 took part in 24 race meetings and it had 16 firsts and seven seconds but of course at many of the meetings it would run in more than one race."*

He went on to say, *"Thank you again for sending me the picture which I shall treasure and do keep in touch. There was an Apps at one of my schools I was at. I think it was Sherborne so perhaps he was your father or some relation."*

His son Robbie told of the time he was at Sherborne looking forward to being met by his father at the end of term in the very first 300SL Mercedes to arrive in the country. He was disappointed when Tony Vandervell arrived to collect his son in a second 300SL!

The B Type Connaught

The B-Type Connaught appeared for the new Formula in 1954 with a fuel-injected Alta engine produced, in conjunction with Harry Weslake, of 2.3- and later 2.5-litres. The design of a new a cylinder head was influenced by the Norton motorcycle engine, and it had a new more stream-lined body. An alternative wind cheating body which had a tail fin and enclosed all four wheels was also tried but not persevered with because of difficulties encountered in obtaining rapid access to the engine compartment during pit stops. There was also a slightly eccentric looking model, quickly nicknamed the "Toothpaste Tube" because that was exactly what it looked like, and it was almost as quickly discarded. Full marks have to be awarded to Connaught for being forward thinking and innovative, not least for its adoption of fuel injection and the team's own wind tunnel. Connaughts certainly enlivened the motor racing scene at a time when no two makes of car in the paddock were ever alike.

In 1955 the B-Type Connaught was equipped with twin-choke Weber carburettors and in October one carved its name in history in the Syracuse Grand Prix.

Rodney Clark had been impressed when he saw Tony Brooks driving a four-year-old Connaught and as a result invited him to drive for the works team.

The Syracuse Grand Prix

Two cars were sent to Syracuse for Tony Brooks and Les Leston to drive and they left England in their transporter, which was a modified bus, a week in advance. When the first practice session took place the cars had still not arrived and so Brooks and Leston had to make do with Vespas to familiarise themselves with the 3.4 mile road circuit. The event would not count towards the World Championship and so the Mercedes Benz team was not there, but the Maserati team was present in force, and two of the latest works cars were driven by Luigi Musso and Luigi Villoresi. The Italians were unaware of the fact that Tony Brooks was about to prove that he was one of the finest racing drivers this country had ever produced and they were not expecting much from his Connaught. The two British cars arrived in time to take part in the second practice session and, to everyone's surprise, Brooks clocked the fastest time of all. On Saturday Musso and Villoresi were determined to uphold the honour of their country come what may and, as a result, occupied the first two places on the starting grid for the race. Brooks, however, was right alongside them on the front row. The order at the end of the first lap was, as might have been expected, Musso, Villoresi and Harry Schell in their three red Maseratis, followed by Brooks and Leston in their green Connaughts. But Brooks was close to Villoresi and Schell and overtook them on the next lap. Then Brooks closed right up to Musso and the two raced round the circuit at record speed. They passed and repassed until Brooks at last established a secure lead and continued to draw ever further away from the Italian car. On lap 55 he established a new lap record at an average speed of 102.36mph and at the end of the race achieved the first win in a Grand Prix by a British driver in a British car since Seagrave won the San Sebastian Grand Prix in his Sunbeam in1924. Musso and Villoresi came second and third and the Connaught was minutely examined by the officials after the race to make sure that the car conformed in every respect to the regulations. The B-Type subsequently became known ever after as the "Syracuse" Connaught, while of course Tony Brooks went on to achieve even greater things with Vanwall and Ferrari.

In the 1950s one watched the steady progression of British racing cars towards the time when they would be able to beat all comers, and this success by Tony Brooks with the Connaught at Syracuse represented a crucial point in their progress.

Archie Scott-Brown in the B-Type 2.5 litre Connaught, at Goodwood on Easter Monday, 1956.

In 1956 I watched a thrilling race at Goodwood between Stirling Moss in his works 250F Maserati, Archie Scott-Brown, of Lister Jaguar fame, in the B-Type Connaught and Mike Hawthorn in the P25 B.R.M. I remember thinking at the time that motor racing could never get better than that! The Connaught held second place as the three cars circulated in close formation but sadly was forced to retire, as was the B.R.M., with fading brakes and a broken engine. According to Stirling Moss, Hawthorn later said that the B.R.M. "had tripled his laundry bills!"

Sadly Connaught was forced to drop out of motor racing in 1957 due to the absence of any major sponsorship. What would have been the future of the marque had it enjoyed adequate funds remains one of the fascinating "ifs and buts" of motor racing.

VANWALL

Guy Anthony Vandervell was the son of Charles Anthony Vanderell who founded C.A.V. the giant electrical company. Tony Vandervell, the son, became the Chairman of Vandervell Products after obtaining the United Kingdom licence for producing Thin Wall bearings. With Alfred Owen and Joseph Lucas, he was one the industrialists who joined the original Trust that backed the B.R.M. project in 1947. Alfred Owen's support for the V16 B.R.M. never flagged but Vandervell had a much more volatile temperament and he was prone to impatience. Raymond Mays said that Vandervell and he "rubbed each other the wrong way" and it is not surprising that Vandervell eventually decided to part company with B.R.M. and to go motor racing on his own.

Vandervell's Green Ferraris

First Tony Vandervell bought a 1.5-litre supercharged Ferrari, which Ken Richardson crashed during the British Grand Prix in 1949. Then, in 1950 he bought a 4.5-litre unsupercharged Ferrari

Mike Hawthorn in the 4.5-litre
Thin Wall Special, winning the
Goodwood Trophy race at
Goodwood in 1953.

which, after being extensively modified and painted green, was called the "Thinwall Special". The name was inscribed in white paint along the sides of its bonnet and it all seemed to me to smack more of Indianapolis than Silverstone. Yet it was a formidable looking machine of vast proportions, dwarfing the little V16 B.R.M. It became locked in conflict with the cars from Bourne in Formula Libre events, Vandervell using the services of Giuseppe Farina, Peter Collins and Mike Hawthorn.

The First Vanwall

Then Vandervell decided to show B.R.M. the way to do it by building his own Grand Prix winner called the Vanwall.

The first "Vanwall Special" was designed by Owen Maddock and built for Vandervell by John Cooper. Vandervell happened to be a director of Norton and the car had a four cylinder 2-litre unsupercharged twin overhead engine developed by Leo Kuzmicki of Norton and ex-B.R.M. designer Eric Richter, from the single cylinder Norton motorcycle engine together with a modified Rolls Royce crankcase.

It became known simply as the "Vanwall" in 1955 when its engine was enlarged to 2.5 litres. Alan Brown drove it in the International Trophy race at Silverstone where it failed to finish and this set the pattern for the season. It had an unpleasing appearance having, at that early stage, a tubular radiator mounted externally along the top of the bonnet. Hawthorn retired the Vanwall at Monaco and Wharton and Schell shared a Vanwall to finish ninth in the British Grand Prix but they were eighteen laps behind the winning Mercedes. Two cars, driven by Schell and Trintignant, also failed to finish the Italian Grand Prix. However Brown came second to the 250F Maserati of Stirling Moss at Goodwood in September. The following month the car again came second to Moss at Aintree driven by Mike Hawthorn.

The 2-litre Vanwall Special, in 1953.

B.G.Apps

The Frank Costin Vanwall

In 1956 Tony Vandervell really got down to business and commissioned Colin Chapman and Lotus to produce an entirely new car. It had a multi-tubular space frame chassis, and an aerodynamically advanced tear drop shaped body with a high tail and sides designed by Frank Costin. Harry Weslake obtained more power from its engine and the car was provided with disc brakes and fuel injection.

Moss won the International Trophy at Silverstone, being released by Maserati for the race, but later that season, with the cars in the hands of Schell and Trintignant, Vandervell had little success. Schell finished fourth in the Belgian Grand Prix at Spa and Schell came tenth in the French Grand Prix after taking over Hawthorn's car, five laps behind the winning Lancia Ferrari of Peter Collins.

1957

Rear leaf springs replaced the coil springs for 1957 and Stirling Moss chose to drive for Vanwall, being joined in the team by Tony Brooks and Stuart Lewis Evans. The cars now developed 280 bhp and Moss won both at Pescara and the Italian Grand Prix at Monza, in each case relegating Fangio's World Championship winning Maserati to second place. At Monza Moss' dominance was such that he could afford to stop for oil and a drink on the 12th lap and then virtually cruise to the end.

Brooks and Moss shared first place at Aintree in the British Grand Prix. After commanding the race from the front Stirling's Vanwall was slowed with magneto problems. He took over Brook's car when it lay in ninth place, as Brook's was in pain from an injured leg after his accident at Le Mans. Moss then steadily gained ground to take the lead from Lewis Evans after the two Lancia Ferraris of Behra and Hawthorn were forced to retire, Behra's with a broken clutch and Hawthorn's with a puncture.

1958

In 1958 the Vanwalls were disadvantaged because new regulations required the use of ordinary pump fuel which reduced their power. In spite of this the Vanwalls won six of the nine events in the World Championship, Stirling Moss winning the Dutch, Portuguese and Moroccan Grands Prix and Tony Brooks the Grands Prix of Belgian, Germany and Italy. Tragically Stuart Lewis Evans died of his burns at Casablanca when, after his engine had seized up, the rear wheels locked, causing it to crash in flames. It was the last race for the World Championship and Mike Hawthorn won the Drivers' Championship for Ferrari by one point from Stirling Moss with Tony Brooks

Stirling Moss winning the Dutch Grand Prix in a Vanwall, in 1958.

in third place. Tony Vandervell had the satisfaction of seeing his Vanwalls win the Constructors' Championship from Ferrari.

After this Tony Vandervell withdrew his team from racing, partly because he was suffered with heart trouble and had received stern warnings from his doctor, but also because he was deeply affected by the loss of Lewis Evans. A new Vanwall did appear in 1959 and it was driven by Tony Brooks. A mid-engined car was built for the Intercontinental Formula for John Surtees to drive in 1962, but there were no further successes.

Tony Vanderell had achieved his object ahead of Raymond Mays and B.R.M., but henceforth the name of Vanwall was only to exist in the history books while the cars were consigned to museums.

Yet, in addition to securing the Constructors' World Championship, a Vanwall, driven by Stirling Moss and Tony Brooks brought to Great Britain its first ever Grand Prix victory on its own soil and, to Formula One, its last successful front-engined racing car.

The 1958 Italian Grand Prix

It is worth recounting how Tony Brooks won the Italian Grand Prix for Vanwall in 1958 defeating the Ferraris once again on their home ground at Monza. He was second in practice to the Vanwall of Moss, with Hawthorn's Ferrari and Lewis Evans Vanwall making up the front row of the grid. Hawthorn's Ferrari had disc brakes and the British driver had also tried the new Dino 256 car. Vanwall experimented with a Perspex cockpit cover on Moss' car, but neither the new Ferrari nor the Vanwall's perspex cover were used in the race.

The three Vanwalls led at the start, pursued by Phil Hill's Ferrari which had come up from seventh place on the grid. The Ferrari was in the lead by the end of the first lap and held this position until being overtaken by Hawthorn on lap five, the two Italian cars being ahead of the three Vanwalls. Then Phil Hill dropped back, so that the order became Hawthorn, Moss, Lewis Evans, Brooks and Behra's B.R.M. Stirling Moss overtook Mike Hawthorn only to be retaken and eventually retired with gearbox troubles on lap 18. Then, when Hawthorn stopped for new tyres it was Phil Hill who went back into the lead, only to lose it when he too had to come in to change the wheels on his Ferrari. All the while Tony Brooks had been moving steadily up the field so that on lap 46 he lay second to Hawthorn with Phil Hill's Ferrari behind him. On lap 60 Brooks passed Hawthorn to take the lead, but he was concerned about the condition of his tyres and watched them anxiously for the remaining laps. Nevertheless he led the two Ferraris of Hawthorn and Hill across the line at the finish after what had been a most enthralling race. The Maserati of the Americans Maston Grergory and Carol Shelby was fourth, Roy Salvadori fifth in a Cooper-Climax and Graham Hill and Cliff Alison sixth and seventh in Lotus-Climaxs. The race was made all the more dramatic by Brooks having been delayed at one point to have the source of smoke which was issuing from the rear of his Vanwall investigated. It was not deemed to be a major problem and he was able to re-enter the race and win. The struggle between the British Vanwalls and the Italian Ferraris must have been enthralling even for any "neutrals" in the crowd!

The 2.5-litre Formula

The 2.5 litre Formula was a spectacular success from the enthusiast's point of view as it saw the return of Mercedes Benz with their W196s, both the streamlined versions and those with open wheels, the D50 Lancias with their highly original side tanks, followed by the Lancia Ferraris, the 250F Maseratis, the P25 B.R.Ms and the Syracuse Connaughts. And of course it saw the introduction of the Coventry-Climax engine which was to bring Cooper and Lotus to the fore.

Motor racing is all about timing. After Vandervell's earlier efforts, the Frank Costin designed Vanwall reached perfection just in time to be a world beater, whereas had circumstances delayed it for a further year, it would have been overwhelmed by the mid-engined Coopers, as was the Aston Martin Grand Prix contender which was seen only briefly in 1959.

PRINCE RAINIER OF MONACO

M ONACO HAS always been closely associated in my mind with motor sport. As a young-ster I listened breathlessly to the reports by Raymond Baxter of the Monte Carlo Rally on the wireless – and to an imaginative youngster the wireless, or radio, had so much more to offer than television ever could! I listened as the British contingent were about to set off across the Channel having driven down from Scotland and, in my sleep, accompanied them as they drove over the narrow roads of the Maritime Alps through snow and ice before dropping down into the warm sunlight of Monte Carlo. Baxter always took a special interest in the progress in partic-ular of ex Bomber Command "Cat's-Eyes" Cunningham who, if my memory serves me correctly, drove a Rolls Royce which was equipped with a cocktail cabinet behind its front seats! I carefully stuck the wonderfully atmospheric pencil sketches of Frank Wootton from *Motor* magazines in my Monte Carlo Rally Scrapbook. Frank Wootton even managed to make a Ford Zephyr look dramatically fast on the mountain roads. I was particularly pleased when Sydney Allard won the Rally in one of his own P2 saloons. I used to go to the London Motor Show each year and always made a bee line for the Allard stand to see the brand new J2 sports cars with their big American V8 engines, motorcycle type mudguards, leather seats and brightly coloured bodywork, and I frequently saw the brand new cars being tested on the road around Clapham Common. Sydney Allard drove a J2 to third place at Le Mans in 1950.

Photograph presented to me, of Prince Rainier and his family, with a portrait of Princess Grace in the background.

Monaco

The Principality of Monaco is no larger than Hyde Park but it has a population in excess of 30,000, one-sixth of them being Monegasque.

In 1227 Francois Grimaldi, who was also known as Frank the Spiteful, took command of its fortress after gaining entrance disguised as a monk. One can imagine the surprise and consternation of its occupants when he removed his hood and produced a sharp sword from under his cloak! The Grimaldis are Europe's oldest ruling family and its coat of arms includes a pair of Friars armed with swords. Somerset Maughan described Monaco as "a sunny spot for shady people" but Prince Rainier, who reigned from 1949 until his death in 2005, turned it into a modern state which is no longer dependent upon the revenue from its casino. His marriage to the American film actress Grace Kelly in 1956 captured the imagination of the world, and everyone was saddened when Princess Grace died in a road accident in 1982 at the age of fifty-one, as was the case when another beautiful princess died tragically some years later in Paris.

The Monaco Grand Prix

The first Monaco Grand Prix was held in 1929 and the first Monte Carlo Rally in 1932. Neither could take place from 1937 until 1948 because of the war and in 1952 the Grand Prix took the

Rudolf Caracciola in his 7.1-litre SSK Mercedes, in the 1929 Monaco Grand Prix.

form of a one hundred lap race for sports cars. The race was not held in 1953. but since then it has taken place each year and has acquired a unique place in the Formula One calendar.

After watching on television Prince Rainier presiding over the prize giving ceremony, I sent him a painting of Graham Hill winning the Monaco Grand Prix in 1964. The Prince, who was also the Duke of Valentinois, the Marquis of Baux, the Count of Carlades, and the Lord of Matignon in addition to one hundred and forty other titles, replied personally on his embossed Palace notepaper in the following way.

> *Dear Reverend,*
> *I should like to thank you personally for your kind letter of March 4th, and for the enclosed painting you performed of the late Graham Hill winning the Monaco Grand Prix in 1964. I am deeply touched by your thoughtful gesture especially since Mr Graham Hill was a man for whom I have always held a great deal of admiration for his courage and determination. Enclosed please find a 1986 Grand Prix poster numbered 00010 and two stickers of the 44th Monaco Grand Prix.*
> *With all best wishes.*

Louis Chiron's Bugatti being pursued by Williams' similar car at Monaco in 1930.

I displayed one of the Monaco stickers in the rear window of my Ford Sierra and when I was at a clergy conference at Old Alresford Place in Hampshire later that year one of my colleagues expressed surprise at seeing it there. When I casually replied, "Yes, Prince Rainier gave it to me," he went away open mouthed and speechless!

I went to Monaco in 1987 with Kath and our children, Wendy and Michael and we walked around the roads which form the circuit each year, including of course the tunnel.

In 1989 I sent Prince Rainier a portrait of Emerson Fittipaldi together with his Lotus and McLaren cars and he enclosed with his reply a recent photograph of himself and Prince Albert which both had autographed, adding at the bottom of his letter with his own pen *"Most sincerely, and congratulations!"*

Castelloti's Lancia followed by Moss and Fangio, in the 1955 Monaco Grand Prix.

In 1994 the Prince asked me to let him know when I would next be visiting his Principality and, as a result of this John Diter, his Private Secretary, booked Kath, Michael and me into the Viking Hotel in Menton the next July. When we arrived at the hotel, after travelling by coach from Nice Airport, we found gifts from the Prince waiting for us in our room, and very shortly afterwards John Diter arrived to welcome us in person. The next day we met him in the Palace and were taken to the Prince's Motor Museum where he left us until we were to meet again for dinner

Niki Lauda winning the Monaco Grand Prix in 1975, with the Ferrari 312 T.

that evening. We walked around the museum until we came to the section devoted entirely to the Grands Prix which contained Louis Chiron's Bugatti, Jackie Stewart's Matra, and Nigel Mansell's Ferrari. Around the walls were Grand Prix posters going back to the first race in 1929 and on either side of the entrance six of the paintings I had sent to the Prince.

Before going to Monaco I had given Prince Rainier a portrait of himself with views of a Graham Hill's B.R.M. and Alain Prost's McLaren. In replying he had written, *"As you do, I fervently hope that this year's race will be a most memorable one, and that the weather will be with us on this very special occasion."* Then he added by hand at the bottom of his letter, *"But I do feel that you should have kept me out of the picture!!"* When we met John Diter told me that the Prince wanted me to repaint that section of the picture and put a third car in it instead.

John Diter told us that he had been with the Prince since his children were born. He had accompanied Princess Grace whenever she went shopping and carried her purse. He had also kept vigil all the while that her body was laying in State.

In 1999 Prince Rainier sent me a photograph of himself and his family with the portrait of Princess Grace behind them and, in a presentation folder which he had signed, a special stamp commemorating his Golden Jubilee as Prince of Monaco.

Also in 1999 the members of my Church in Bournemouth organised a concert by the Morriston Orpheus Choir to celebrate my twenty-one years as the vicar of the parish. To my absolute astonishment a message from Prince Rainier was read out to the audience which went as follows.

> *"It gives me great pleasure to send you a message of congratulations and good wishes as a fitting tribute to your 21 years of service in Bournemouth and All Saints, at the same time, a celebration of your return to good health.*
>
> *Only recently have I received your latest painting to add to the many you have sent me in the past years. They are exhibited in my personal collection of vintage vehicles and admired by a large number of tourists from all over the world.*
>
> *Thank you, dear Reverend, for all of them.*
>
> *I send warm greetings to you, your dear wife Kathleen and your family."*

Prince Rainer had a heart bypass the next year and in June 2000 he wrote, *"I am glad to know that you have fully recovered from your quadruple heart bypass operation and I thank you for your kind prayers and good wishes for my health."* He added by hand underneath, *"I am recuperating slowly, steadily and quietly. All the best."*

Having been privileged to correspond with Prince Rainier over so many years, I felt a profound sense of personal loss when he passed away on April 6 2005 at the age of 81.

THE COMMENTATORS

I HOPE THAT the excellent Martin Brundle, Mark Blundell, Jonathan Palmer and others will forgive me if I say that the two motor racing commentators who come instantly to my mind are Raymond Baxter and Murray Walker.

RAYMOND BAXTER

Before the days of television Raymond Baxter had to paint the scene in words to unseeing listeners and he sometimes only had a couple of minutes to do it in before the start of a race. Yet in cultured tones and finely turned phrases he managed to convey so much about the cars and the drivers. He

Raymond Mays in E.R.A. R4D at Shelsley Walsh in 1948, after posting the fastest time.

B. G. Apps '86

had flown Spitfires throughout the North African Campaign in the Second World War and become a Squadron Leader. He had dive bombed the launching sites of the dreaded V2 rockets and was twice mentioned in despatches. So he easily related to the many motor racing drivers of the late forties and early fifties who had also been through the war and he knew many of them on a personal basis. He thoroughly understood the sport, the drivers and the cars.

As a broadcaster Raymond Baxter commentated on the State Funerals of King George VI, Sir Winston Churchill and Lord Mountbatten of Burma and the Coronation of our Queen. So he was able to bring some gravitas and authority to motor racing at a time when it struggled for a place in the national consciousness alongside football and other sports.

Raymond Baxter was enthusiastic about motor racing, rallying and aviation, and with the B.B.C. he reported on fourteen Monte Carlo Rallies. His first was in 1950, and he competed in the Rally the following year as the co-driver of Gordon Wilkins in a works Jowett Jupiter. Can I ever forgive the Ford Motor Company for causing the demise of Jowett when it took over Briggs Motor Bodies in Eastleigh and discontinued the production of bodies for the Javelin and Jupiter cars? Baxter drove in later Monte Carlo Rallies with a Sunbeam Rapier and a B.M.C. Mini Cooper and he also took part in the Tulip and Alpine Rallies.

In later years Raymond Baxter became more famous for Presenting "Tomorrow's World" and "The Tomorrow's World Time Machine" on television, but he never turned his back on the past and was the Admiral of the Association of Dunkirk Little Ships, owning one of the "little ships" himself.

Before the Christmas of 1986 I sent Raymond Baxter a painting of Raymond Mays, with cigarette in his mouth, driving his black E.R.A. R4D down the hill of Shelsley Walsh in 1948, after establishing the fastest time of the day.

He was clearly delighted with the gift and on December 12 1986 wrote as follows:

> *Your generous and unique gesture has come as one of the highlights of my Christmas, and occupies a commanding position in the sitting room a top the serried ranks of the complete works of Dickens!*
>
> *You may be interested to learn that it thereby occasioned interest and comment from our usual stream of Christmas callers, several of whom, being motor racing buffs, were challenged to identify car and driver. Two got it right. The others were too young. One of the winners was my old mate of many ventures Tony Mays. I wonder if you knew him.*
>
> *But apart from all that the consensus was that it is a clever and striking painting, and one which will duly go to the library with my other small collection of motoring, boating, and flying pictures. (That sounds very grand. It's not really.)*
>
> *It was really a charming gesture on your part, for which I am truly grateful.*
>
> *Thank you very much, and may I reciprocate your good wishes for the New Year? You have given me a delightful reminder of days which, though, long gone, are rich in happy memories. I'm sure I share with you the hope that the years to come will be as rewarding to the next generation as they were to us.*
>
> *With every good wish and thanks again.*
>
> > *Yours sincerely,*
> > *Raymond Baxter.*

I wrote to Raymond Baxter again in October 2003 after hearing his commentary of the last flight of the Concorde, to say how pleased I was to hear his voice on air again.

He replied thanking me for my letter and said that he was particularly pleased that it was Concorde which had revived my memories of our original contact in 1986 – which was a year after he and his wife had moved to Henley on Thames. He added, *"And good gracious, that was literally an era ago!"*

MURRAY WALKER

Raymond Baxter described himself once as Raymond Baxter B.M.W., and went on to explain that the letters stood for "Before Murray Walker!"

Murray Walker served in the Army during the war as a Tank Commander and afterwards was employed by Dunlop. He was also involved in the advertising world and was associated with the famous slogan, "A Mars a day helps you work rest and play." His father Graham Walker raced motorcycles and commented for the B.B.C. on motorcycle events and it was this that brought Murray into close contact with motor sport. Following in his father's footsteps, he won a gold medal in an International Six Day Trial in 1949 and eventually did two hundred broadcasts for the B.B.C. on the Isle of Man TT races.

The B.B.C. asked Murray to take part in their broadcast of the British Grand Prix for racing cars at Silverstone in 1949 and, after Raymond Baxter, he became the voice of motor racing on B.B.C. Television as Formula One gained rapidly in popularity, ably assisted by the World Champion racing driver James Hunt. Martin Brundle became his co presenter after the sad death of James Hunt and by this time it seemed that the voice of Murray Walker was essential for the full enjoyment of any race.

He was passionate and informative, with his voice revving away in time with the cars. He became famous for his Murrayisms such as, "anything can happen and probably will" and "Unless I am very much mistaken – and I am very much mistaken". They enhanced the impact of his commentaries and they were no more errors than are the asymmetric features of a Picasso masterpiece.

Perhaps his experience in advertising helped him to find the right word for the occasion but he became, both on the B.B.C. and I.T.V. the master of his craft.

I decided to send Murray Walker a painting of Tazio Nuvolari winning the Italian Grand Prix at Monza in 1938 in the D-Type Auto Union as I felt sure that Nuvolari, with his motor cycling background, would have been one of his foremost racing heroes.

Tazio Nuvolari winning the Italian Grand Prix in his Auto Union, in 1938.

In his reply in May 1986 he wrote of what he described as my uncanny perception of his interest in Nuvolari.

He wrote:

"He really is my motor racing hero (even above Fangio and Moss) and I have had the very great privilege of meeting him, watching him race and receiving one of his personal "Tortoise" charms. A great friend of my father was an Englishman who married a German girl as a result of being a member of the British Army of Occupation of the Rhine after World War One. He made a lot of money in the car business in Cologne and amused himself by acting as Interpreter for the Auto Union and Mercedes Benz teams whenever they went to English speaking countries like the U.K, America and South Africa. As a result of that I tagged along as a teenager when they went to Donington and met all the greats of the day – Caracciola, Rosemeyer, Lang, Varzi, Nuvolaro et al. I was awestruck then and awestruck now at my good fortune!"

So you really could not have chosen a more welcome subject and I shall proudly feature your framed painting in my study.

Incidentally, when my father finished his motorcycle racing career he became Sales Director of Rudge Whitworth and, as such, supplied many racing Rudges to Enzo Ferrari who, at that time, ran both car (Alfa Romeo) and motorcycle (Rudge) teams under the Scuderia Ferrari banner. One of his riders was Nuvolari!

Tazio Nuvolari winning the 1935 German Grand Prix in his Alfa Romeo.

In 1994 I sent Murray Walker a further painting of Nuvolari, this time winning the German Grand Prix in 1935 in his P3 Alfa Romeo. It was a great day for the Italian driver but left Manfred von Brauchitsch distraught, his tyre having failed on the last lap when he was in sight of victory. In his reply on April 18th 1994 Murray wrote:

The new season seems to be starting well and I am mightily relieved that Senna and Williams have not walked away with the opening races as I expected them to. I think they will get themselves together from Imola onwards when we reach the fast European tracks, but with Senna having scored no points in the first two races it means that there will be plenty to maintain our interest and enthusiasm whilst he is trying to catch up. I think Ferrari will do better as the season progresses too, so we have got plenty to look forward to.

When I was in Brazil I spent a morning with Senna in his personal sixteen-storey, glass-clad skyscraper from which he controls his very successful business empire and it was a fascinating experience. His office, which is full of memorabilia like his three World Championship awards,

Ayrton Senna winning the Portuguese Grand Prix in 1985, in his Lotus-Renault 97T.

his three autosprint "stick men" trophies for being Driver of the Year, superb models of his race cars and various other bits of memorabilia, looks out over Sao Paulo (which is about the best thing to do there!) and we had what was, for me, a truly rewarding conversation. He is immensely intense, does not suffer fools gladly and tends not to crack too many jokes but he is a very nice chap. Even if he wasn't I could forgive him a lot for his overall talent and the pleasure his driving and professionalism have given me over the years. And if you, like everyone else in the U.K if my mail is anything to go by, wondered why I had suddenly started calling him Eye-airton it was because I had become uncomfortably aware of the fact that that is what he likes. But now, having apparently offended half the U.K. I'm cravenly returning to my old sloppy Englishman's mispronunciation!

I have an undated Christmas card from him in which he wrote "To my friend Murray with my grateful thanks for all your help with my career." Very impressive but I don't tell many of the people who look at me in awe that he sent it to me at the end of his first year in Formula Ford! His well-deserved personal situation, for which he has fought very hard indeed and to achieve which he has literally risked his life during every second that he was working, contrasts vividly with the many thousands in Sao Paulo, Rio and many other places in Brazil, who exist in unspeakable hovels called Favelas which have no electricity, no water and no sanitation. I know he does a great deal for local charities but he will not even speak about it, let alone seek publicity. For that I admire him a great deal.

Tragically Ayrton Senna died just thirteen days later on May 1st during the Imola Grand Prix when his Williams suddenly left the circuit at high speed and a front suspension strut pierced his helmet. It seemed strange that something had prompted Murray Walker to write to me so fully about him less than a fortnight before.

JAGUARS AND ASTON MARTINS

Le Mans

1950

Jaguar made its first appearance at Le Mans in 1950 with three relatively standard XK120 cars driven by Clark/Haines, who finished twelfth, Whitehead/Marshall, who came fifteenth and Johnson/Hadley, who retired in the twenty-third hour after running in seventh place. Of David Brown's three Aston Martin DB1s, the car driven by Abecassis/Macklin finished fifth, that of Brackenbury/Parnell sixth, and the third, driven by Fairman/Thompson, retired after three hours.

1951

The team from Coventry returned in 1951 with the new lighter and more powerful C-Type Jaguars. Stirling Moss led the race in the rain after three laps, breaking the lap record several times and, after six hours, the other two Jaguars were running second and third. Then mechanical troubles intervened and the Moss/Fairman and Johnson/Biondetti Jaguars retired with broken oil pipes. The drivers of the remaining Jaguar, Peter Walker and Peter Whitehead, being well clear of the rest of the field, were instructed to circulate at reduced speed to finish the race in first place. The three Aston Martin DB2s driven by Macklin/Thompson, Abecassis/Shaw-Taylor and Parnell/Hampshire finished third, fifth and seventh.

British entries that year also included Healeys, Frazer Nashs, Bentleys, Jowetts, Allards and M.G.s.

1952

1952 was disastrous for Jaguar. Stirling Moss had been impressed with the speed of the Ferraris and Mercedes Benz cars and believed that the Jaguar needed to increase that of their cars. The new cars looked magnificent with lower bodies and elongated streamlined bonnets to reduce wind resistance, although Duncan Hamilton told me later that they could have won the race with the previous year's cars, bearing in mind that, in 1952 they had the advantage of disc brakes. There was insufficient time to test the new cooling system before the race and it became apparent in practice that the modified fronts would cause the Jaguars to overheat. Although larger radiators were hastily fitted all three cars were forced to retire early on in the race. The Whitehead/Stewart car retired in the second hour with a blown cylinder head gasket; the Moss/Walker car retired in the third hour with a broken big end while running in eighth place and that of Rolt/Hamilton retired an hour later with another blown cylinder head gasket.

David Brown brought his new DB3 Aston Martins to Le Mans in 1952 with 2.6-litre W. O. Bentley designed engines in cars with tubular chasses designed by Professor Robert Eberhorst.

They were driven by Macklin/Collins, Parnell/Thompson and Mann/Morris Goodall. The Collins/Macklin car ran in fourth place at one time but all three retired in the course of the race.

This was the year when Mercedes Benz returned to the sport in force with three new 300SLs. Alfred Neubauer, the team manager who had guided them through the 1930s, calculated what would be the minimum speed with which the race could be won and, and they set off precisely at that speed, regardless of anyone else. The plan almost failed as Pierre Levegh, having driven his Talbot throughout without handing over to his co driver, had a clear lead after twenty-three hours. Then, after nursing what turned out to be a sick engine for most of the race, Levegh's crankshaft broke with only fifty minutes to go. The Mercedes team then took over the first two places, while the Press unfairly accused Levegh of having wrecked his engine by changing into the wrong gear through sheer exhaustion!

1953

In 1953 the big 4.1-litre Ferraris were the ones to beat, but Jaguar returned with three C-Types looking very much as they had done two years before although they were lighter and of course had disc brakes. David Brown had a team of new curvaceous DB3S cars and, in all, no less than eighteen manufacturers entered cars for the event. It was racing at its very best.

Duncan Hamilton and Tony Rolt were to drive car number 18 but on the eve of the race they learned that they had been disqualified on a technicality. It so happened that, through no fault of their own, two cars had been on the circuit with their number 18 at the same time and for that reason they were to be excluded. Both drivers decided to drown their sorrows in a local hostelry, although Tony Rolt strenuously denied later that they had indulged excessively. Whatever was the case they were then told that they could race after all and many cups of black coffee were consumed before the start!

Sydney Allard led initially in one of his own cars and then Moss took the lead from Villoresi's 4.5-litre Ferrari before falling back through the field with fuel starvation. Then Rolt took the lead and after several hours the car was far in front of the Villoresi/Hawthorn Ferrari.

Villoresi's Ferrari leading the Jaguars of Moss and Rolt at Le Mans in 1953.

Hamilton's C-Type Jaguar leading Ascari's Ferrari at Le Mans, in 1953.

As Hamilton was driving down the long Mulsanne straight at 150mph a bird hit his windscreen, breaking much of it away and forcing him to lean constantly to the left to take cover from the force of the air that passed over his car. In spite of this he and Rolt won the race for Jaguar, and England in the year of the Coronation. The Stirling Moss/Peter Walker car finished second and the third car driven by Peter Whitehead/Jimmy Stewart was fourth.

Hamilton winning the 1953 Le Mans race.

The new Aston Martin DB3Ss designed by Willie Watson were driven by Parnell and Collins, Salvadori and Abecassis, and Poore and Thompson and they disappointingly failed to finish the race.

Many years later Duncan Hamilton invited me to see his winning C-Type Jaguar which he had recently acquired from Briggs Cunningham in America and which had recently undergone a complete restoration. His son Adrian showed the car to me in their garage in Bagshot. Duncan told me that when he was practicing for Le Mans in the 50s he used an advertising board at the side of one point in the circuit as a guide in changing down a gear for a corner. One day he did this as usual but found that he was approaching the corner too fast and failed to get round. Afterwards he discovered that someone had moved the board several yards further on!

1954

In 1954 the D-Type Jaguar appeared at Le Mans. It was of monocoque construction, aerodynamically efficient and complete with a tail fin. Sadly the race was marred for them as particles of sand contaminated their fuel. They were up against 4.9-litre Ferraris driven by Froilan Gonzales and Luigi Villoresi. Gonzales led initially but was overtaken by Moss who was then delayed by miss-firing. The D Type of Moss/Walker retired after an eventful race, as did that of Whitehead/Wharton. However the Jaguar driven by Hamilton and Rolt began to catch the leading Ferrari in heavy rain, its fuel problems having been overcome with a change of plugs and a new petrol filter. Then, in drying conditions, Gonzales was able to make better use of the Ferrari's superior power and the Jaguar finished just two miles behind.

In a letter afterwards Tony Rolt reminded me that he and Duncan Hamilton had *"only missed first place by two and a half minutes."* He went on to write, *"Yes, 1953 was certainly a great year and our win was not entirely due to the disc brakes, as is often said, as quite a lot of the opposition had a lot more power, and the C-Type was not particularly fast down the straight."*

The Aston Martin DB3Ss of Parnell and Salvadori retired with mechanical problems while those of Collins/Bira and Whitehead/Stewart both crashed.

The Rolt/Hamilton D-Type Jaguar at Le Mans in 1954.

The Tragedy in 1955

1955 witnessed the dreadful accident involving Mike Hawthorn's Jaguar, Lance Macklin's Austin Healey and Pierre Levegh's Mercedes Benz 300SLR which had been fitted with a large air brake to compensate for not have discs. Fangio's Mercedes and Hawthorn's long-nosed D-Type had circulated in close formation as though they were re-enacting their famous duel in the 1953 French Grand Prix. Then, as Hawthorn turned into his pits at speed, Macklin swerved to avoid him and was hit by Levegh's Mercedes which literally then flew into the crowd, killing the driver and eighty spectators. Fangio managed to squeeze past Macklin on his other side and said afterwards that Levegh had saved his life by raising his hand in warning a split second before the impact. The Mercedes team withdrew and Mike Hawthorn, although devastated by the incident, won the race with the D-Type Jaguar, but no one could take any pleasure from the result.

The Aston Martin of Collins/Frere finished in second place and those of Brooks/Riseley Pritchard and Salvadori/Walker retired with mechanical problems.

Before the accident which caused the loss of so many lives Peter Collins and Roy Salvadori were enjoying their race. Roy's words are recorded by Chris Nixon in *Mon Ami Mate.*

> *"John Wyer had given us strict instructions not to dice with each other and whatever order we were in at the end of the first lap was to be maintained. I made a better start than Pete, but within a couple of laps he was right with me and we had a most God-almighty dice. All round the circuit we were passing and re-passing, pushing each other through the corners and having a wonderful time. Peter was laughing and waving at me, (giving me two fingers, that is!) and we were really going terribly quickly but we always got our positions right as we went past the pits, with me in the lead.*
>
> *Then I lost it coming out of Arnage. I spun right round, Peter went past and from then on he had every right to stay in front. He could have told John that I had spun and said, 'What was I supposed to do – wait for him?' But that's exactly what he did – he gave me two fingers and let me go by again. He never mentioned it to John and neither did I, because that was exactly the kind of thing he was trying to avoid – my spin could have involved Pete and we could have lost both cars. That was how nice a guy he was."*

1956

The Le Mans pits straight was modified in 1956 to minimise the possibility of another tragedy. An Ecurie Ecosse D Type Jaguar, driven by Sanderson/Flockhart won the race and the Aston Martin DB3S of Moss/Collins finished second.

The works Jaguar of Hawthorn/Bueb was sixth while the other two works Jaguars of Frere/Titterington and Fairman/Wharton were eliminated in a first lap incident.

An entirely new Aston Martin DBR1/250 driven by Brooks/Parnell retired in the last hour and the DB3S of Walker/ Salvadori crashed up side down, fortunately without serious injury to its driver.

A further D-Type Jaguar entered by L'Equipe Nationale Belge and driven by Swaters/Rouselle finished in fourth place.

1957

This was to be the last year for Jaguars at Le Mans for a long time. Again it was an Ecurie Ecosse D-Type driven by Flockhart/Bueb that won while another, driven by Sanderson/Lawrence came second. An Equipe Nationale Belge car came fourth and another D-Type driven by Hamilton/Gregory finished in sixth place.

David Brown brought along two DBR1s and a DBR2 all of which sadly failed to finish. The DBR2, driven by Peter and Graham Whitehead retired in the eighth hour, the Salvadori/Leston car in the tenth hour and the Brooks/Cunningham Reid in the twelfth hour.

1958

The Moss/Brabham Aston Martin DBR1 led for the two hours before retiring. That of Salvadori/Lewis Evans retired during the fourth hour, while Brooks and the Aston driven by Brooks/

Trintignant retired in the fifteenth hour after running in third place. The race was won by the Ferrari of Olivier Gendebien and Phil Hill.

Roy Salvadori winning Le Mans in 1959, with the DBR1 Aston Martin.

1959

1959 proved to be David Brown's year at last. Three DBR1s faced the lighter and faster works Ferraris but Stirling Moss in his Aston took an early lead, followed by the two Ferraris. After the first hour Jean Behra led in his Ferrari and drew away but then Moss retook the lead when the Ferrari came in to refuel. Their places were exchanged again but eventually Behra's car dropped back leaving the Moss/Fairman car in the lead with Gendebien's Ferrari in second place and the Salvadori/Shelby Aston third. Moss retired in the sixth hour and during the night Gendebien was ahead of the Astons by three laps until, at 11am, he pitted with overheating problems. The gap narrowed as the Aston Martin of Salvadori/Shelby overhauled it and then the Ferrari had to be withdrawn. Salvadori had driven fourteen of the twenty-four hours and Shelby took over for the last two hours. The winning speed was 112.57 mph and the Aston driven by Trintignant/Frere was second, two hundred miles ahead of the third car, a privately entered Ferrari. Victory had come at last to David Brown, after eleven years.

Roy Salvadori

Le Mans in 1959 must surely stand as the pinnacle of Roy Salvadori's motor racing career. He was one of the great British racing drivers and had he driven a works 250F Maserati instead of a

Signed photograph of Roy Salvadori.

privately owned one, or had the Grand Prix Aston Martin proved to be competitive, he would have gained greater distinction.

The Goodwood Nine Hours

Aston Martins did well in the Goodwood Nine Hours - whereas good fortune always eluded the Jaguars in this unique event.

1952

The three C-Type Jaguars of Moss/Walker, Rolt/Hamilton and Whitehead/Stewart were ranged against the DB3 Aston Martins of Parnell/Thompson, Abecassis/Poore and Collins/Griffiths. Rolt led at the start and then Parnell but, after three hours, the Rolt/Hamilton C-Type was in the lead. Then, when Parnell's car came into the pits to refuel it was suddenly engulfed in flames and two of the Aston Martin mechanics had to be taken to hospital with burns. After this the Moss/Walker Jaguar led from the Rolt/Hamilton car with Collins and Griffiths in third place. Then Salvadori took the lead in a privately entered Ferrari but found that his starter jammed and the race was won by the DB3 of Collins and Griffiths, followed by the Cole/Graham Whitehead 2.7-litre Ferrari.

1953

It seemed that Jaguars would get their own back in 1953 as they led for eight of the nine hours but, when falling oil pressure sidelined the Moss/Walker and the Rolt/Hamilton C-Types, Eric Thompson led in the new DBS. Griffiths overtook the remaining Whitehead/Stewart Jaguar so that the Aston Martins took the first two places.

When Peter Collins won the Tourist Trophy at Dundrod later in the year and I remember the B.B.C. radio commentator remarking on the excellent road holding of the DB3S, saying that when it came to cornering it was "all my eye and Aston Martin!"

1955

The Goodwood Nine Hours Race was not held in 1954 and the last race in the series took place in 1955. There were no works Jaguars but Hamilton and Rolt borrowed a works D-Type to take

The Walker/Poore Aston Martin DB3S, during the Goodwood Nine Hours in 1955.

in the Astons of Parnell/Salvadori, Poore/Walker and Collins/Brooks. Hawthorn's works Ferrari led the three Aston Martins at the start but was delayed at the pits through having to use side jacks to change the wheels. It retired on lap 18 with mechanical problems. The Collins/Brooks Aston was delayed with misfiring and the Ecurie Ecosse Jaguar of Titterington/Sanderson led until delayed by repairs to a headlamp. Eventually the Aston Martins of Poore/Walker and Collins/Brooks finished in first and third positions with the D-Type Jaguar separating them.

The Nine Hour races at Goodwood had not been hugely popular as many of the spectators, not being genuine enthusiasts, lost interest after dark and drifted off home. For the rest it brought something of the excitement of Le Mans to this country.

Jaguar's return to Le Mans

Jaguars returned to Le Mans in 1984 with the XJR-5 in a serious attempt to repeat their earlier successes but they were reminded that success does not come easily at Le Mans. Their two cars reached speeds of up to 212 mph on the Mulsanne Straight but both retired before the end of the race. In 1985 one Jaguar finished in thirteenth place while a second car again retired. Their performance in 1986 was more promising as the Warwick/Cheever/Schlesser car was in second place when a blown tyre caused its retirement. The other two cars also retired. In 1987 the XJR-8LM led the race for three hours and was lying second when a blown head gasket caused its retirement.

Victory in 1988

Then, victory returned to Jaguar at last when, in 1988 the Jaguar XJR-9 LM of Lammers/Dumfries/Wallace came first at an average speed of 137.74 mph.

The three drivers signed my painting which celebrated their success in the pits at Brands Hatch later that year. Johnny Dumfries had sent me three tickets for the 1000 Kilometres Race at Brands Hatch and I went with Kath and Michael. He phoned me later that evening after the race to ask

Johnny Dumfries with my son, Michael.

Johnny Dumfries, now the
Earl of Bute, holding the
painting which he and his co-
drivers signed.

The Lammers/Dumfries/
Wallace Jaguar XJR-9 LM,
winning the Le Mans race in
1988.

me how I had enjoyed the day. It was a splendid occasion marred only by the fact that his car caught fire and the race had been won by one of the Sauber Mercedes Benz C9s.

Derek Bell won at Le Mans in 1975 in a Ford but his later impressive series of wins in '81, '82, '86 and '87 were in Porsches and when I rather cheekily expressed some regret that he had not won with a Jaguar he replied that he *"had not received the call!"*

THE AMERICANS

Briggs Cunningham

Briggs Cunningham brought two Cadillacs to Le Mans in 1950. One was a very standard looking Coupe de Ville which he drove with Phil Waters and the other had an open streamlined body and was nicknamed "Le Monstre". They finished ninth and eleventh. Next Cunningham decided to build his own cars which were called Cunningham C-1s and had Cadillac engines. A team of three C-2Rs were built for Le Mans in 1951 with modified 5.424 Chrysler engine, painted white with blue stripes. They failed to finish but came first second and fourth at Watkins Glen later in the year. In 1952 one of his C-4Rs led at Le Mans before retiring in the eighth hour and another, driven by him and Bill Spear finished in fourth place. Cunningham C-4Rs finished third and

The C-2R Cunningham at Le Mans in 1951.

B. G. Apps '87

seventh in 1953. In 1954 a new C-5R finished third and a C-4R seventh but the next year a team of C-6Rs failed to finish.

Briggs Cunningham wrote to me in March 1987.

Dear Revd. Apps,

I just received the very nice painting of the Cunningham C-2R at Le Mans you so kindly sent me. Thank you so much, and I would love to have it for my photo and picture collection. I do not have one of these particular cars in the collection, as we sold all three of them at the season's end, and built the new C-4R model for 1953, which was an improvement all round. I do believe there are 2 of the C-2R models still running, and one was cut up by us after being in a bad wreck. One car is in this country, and the second one was sold at auction in England just last fall I believe, to a French owner living in Monaco. They were the first sports-racing cars we built in our own shops in Florida, and we used the new Chrysler Hemi engines in them. They were strong cars; very reliable; but heavy.

Sincerely yours, and keep on painting!

Briggs Cunningham

A 5.4-litre Cunningham C5R.

Dan Gurney

Dan Gurney drove for Ferrari, B.R.M. and Porsche in Formula One and, with his own Company, All American Races Inc, based at Rye in Sussex, he built and raced the Grand Prix Eagle cars. They were dark blue with a white stripe and his first car, which appeared in 1966 had a Coventry-Climax engined Eagle in 1966. The following year he won the Belgian Grand Prix driving his V12 Weslake engined Eagle. The long nose of his cars vaguely resembled an Eagle's beak and had to be removed before the car could be rolled down the ramp from its transporter. Eagles dominated the Indianapolis 500 races at one point in the 1970s. At Indianapolis in 1973 there were no less than sixteen Eagles, two of which finished in first and second places, and in 1974 eight of the first ten cars were Eagles.

He wrote to me in 1992.

Dear Bryan,

Thank you for your painting. I am honoured to receive it and appreciate your thinking of me. To answer your question, I'd have to say the car I enjoyed driving the most was a winning car. A win just seems to make any car look terrific. Our 1967 Eagle Gurney-Weslake was very special. The old bird cage Maser that I shared with my hero Stirling Moss was a good one. The Brabham F-1 car was good.

Dan Gurney and his Eagle Weslake, winning the Belgian Grand Prix, at Spa, in 1967.

CMC Model of the 'Old Birdcage Maser' that Dan Gurney shared with Stirling Moss.

Currently, we are racing two new AAR designed and built Eagle MK-III G.T.P. cars in the International Motor Sports Association (I.M.S.A) Camel GT series. Our drivers are Juan Fangio II and P.J.Jones. We finished 3rd and 4th in the G.T.P class at the 24 Hours of Dsaytona, where Juan qualified on the pole and set the fastest lap of the race. I'm still very much involved in the racing business as you can see. We currently have over 95 people working here at AAR and there are not many dull moments. My family, 5 boys and 1 girl and wife are all apparently healthy. I recently became a grandfather for the third time.

Thanks again for the painting. It was very kind of you!

All the best and God bless you. Dan Gurney.

Phil Hill

Phil Hill won the Belgian and Italian Grands Prix in a shark-nosed Tipo 156 Ferrari in 1961 and became the first American World Champion racing driver. After I had sent him a painting of him in the car at Monza he phoned from Santa Monica, California to thank me. Kath received the call and had to tell him that I was out at that time taking the Sacrament to the sick, so he said that he would phone again in a couple of hours. He was true to his word and we had a long chat. He also wrote to me later to say that he had received the painting back from the framers and that it looked very nice.

Phil Hill's Ferrari T180 156 in the 1961 Monaco Grand Prix.

SIR STIRLING MOSS

I T HAPPENED when I was putting my new 1.8-litre Morris Marina through its paces. It was a modest family saloon but capable of a moderately respectable turn of speed, until British Leyland ran out of spare parts for its gearbox! What happened was that a Volvo police car pulled

up in front of me and the inevitable question that followed was, "Who do you think you are, Stirling Moss?" It indicated the unique place that Stirling has held in the public consciousness from the early 1950s. I would have felt less well qualified to write this book did I not know Stirling Moss and had I not seen him race. I can boast that I have seen Stirling driving Cooper 500s and Keifts, H.W.M.s, XK120 and C-Type Jaguars, his two Cooper Altas and the G-Type E.R.A., an Aston Martin DB3S, a Ferrari 250GTO, a works Maserati 250F and many others. I marvel at Martin Brundle's ability to judge between the driving skills of two drivers as they circulate at lightning speed, almost completely hidden from sight within the comparatively safe cocoons of their twenty-first century racing cars, but the skill of Stirling Moss was clear for all to see and appreciate. He was the epitome of cool as, with his arms outstretched to the steering wheel, like Giuseppe Farina, he made his cars appeared to float smoothly around corners with a minimum of drama, seeming to be slower, instead of very much faster, than all the others. He has said that he cultivated Farina's arms-length style so as to fool his competitors into thinking that it was easy for him. If so, he fooled the rest of us too! Early on I was presumptuous enough to ask Raymond Mays to invite Stirling to

Stirling Moss winning the 1961 Monaco Grand Prix.

drive the V16 B.R.M. but it wasn't long before every team wanted him. It was great for motor racing that someone so young was also so talented and yet so mature at the wheel of any racing car.

Moss drove in events around Europe with the works H.W.M. team and, after winning the Tourist Trophy at Dundrod with Tommy Wisdom's aluminium-bodied Jaguar XK120 in 1950, he joined the works Jaguar team. He was first in his class in the Tourist Trophy race in 1953 driving a C-Type. Wanting to drive British cars, Moss drove the G-Type E.R.A., an A-Type Connaught, and two specially built Cooper Altas. His loyalty to H.W.M. cost him an opportunity to drive for Ferrari. When, in 1954, he eventually became reconciled to the view that he would have to drive a foreign car to keep up with the best, and, following the advice of Alfred Neubauer, he bought a 250F Maserati. It was finished in British Racing Green and wore a Union Jack and horseshoe, and he came third in the Belgian Grand Prix behind Fangio's works car and Trintignant's Ferrari. The next month saw the triumphant return of Mercedes Benz to Formula One and Moss did enough in the course of 1954 to persuade Mercedes Benz to offer him a car for 1955. In May he won the Mille Miglia with Dennis Jenkinson as his navigator, having covered the 1597 kilometres of public roads in ten hours.

In Formula One the famous Fangio/Moss train was set in motion with the W196s and Stirling says that he learned a great deal from the master driving so closely behind him for race after race. Then at Aintree for the British Grand Prix he overtook Fangio and stretched his lead to 12 seconds, breaking the lap record in the process. Fangio caught up, but it was Moss who crossed the line first by less than a car's length. Moss also won the Tourist Trophy for Mercedes Benz with the 300SLR in September 1955, after an exploding rear tyre had torn away a portion of its bodywork. He and Peter Collins won the Targa Florio in Sicily in spite of the fact that the 300SLR had an unscheduled excursion off the road at one point.

At the end of 1955, following the Le Mans tragedy, Mercedes Benz pulled out of racing and

Signed photograph of Stirling Moss with the W196 Mercedes Benz, at Monaco in 1955.

Stirling went to Maserati, having turned down offers from the B.R.M., Connaught and Vanwall teams. One of the reasons for this, as Menard and Vassal explain in *Stirling Mos: The Champion Without a Crown*, was that he preferred not to compete with either of his friends Collins or Hawthorn while driving in the same teams. I saw Stirling win the Glover Trophy at Goodwood in the scarlet works Maserati, but it was with a Vanwall that he won the International Trophy Race at Silverstone, before embarking on the full Championship series with the Maserati. He won the Monaco and Italian Grands Prix and finished second to Fangio's Lancia Ferrari in the World Championship. Moss had also finished second in the 1000 kilometre's sports car race at Monza in the 2 litre Maserati 200S and second, with Collins at Le Mans driving an Aston Martin DB3S.

For 1957 Moss joined Vanwall with Tony Brooks and Stuart Lewis Evans, but he also competed in the Mille Miglia, with Dennis Jenkinson, driving a 4.5-litre V8 Maserati. Their race ended when the brake pedal snapped, and the race itself was stopped for all time when the Ferrari of Alfonso de Portago crashed with fatal consequences for himself and a number of spectators. With Vanwall Moss won the Pescara and Italian Grands Prix, and with Brooks the British Grand Prix and he finished second again in the World Championship to Fangio who, this time, had been driving a Maserati.

The first race in the 1958 calendar was the Argentinian Grand Prix and, in the absence of Vanwall, Moss

Signed painting of Stirling Moss winning the Monaco Grand Prix in a Maserati 250F, in 1956.

Stirling Moss winning the 1957 British Grand Prix in a Vanwall.

scored an historic David versus Goliath win with Rob Walker's little 2-litre Cooper Climax against the might of the 2.5-litre works Ferraris and Maseratis.

The extraordinary partnership of Walker and Moss was very special in the history of motor racing and it proved that, even at that comparatively late stage in the development of motor racing, a privateer could still beat the professional teams. In *Stirling Moss: My Cars, My Career* Rob Walker wrote that he and Stirling never had any contracts and that it was all done by a "gentleman's agreement".

There was a great bond between Walker and Moss, and Rob Walker, like Stirling, was a great character. Robbie Walker recalled at his father's Memorial Service that Rob had once owned a French car which was unusual in that all its forward gears could also be operated in reverse. One day he decided to try it out and he reversed through all the gears at high speed until he ended up in a ditch. When he returned the next day to inspect the damage, a man who was standing by the wrecked car scratching his head, told him that he had seen it driving backwards at sixty miles an hour. Rob Walker merely advised him that he should take more water with it!

Moss won the Dutch Portuguese and Moroccan Grands Prix for Vanwall, finishing second again in the World Championship, with one point less than Hawthorn who had driven for Ferrari.

In 1958 Moss won more Grands Prix than Mike Hawthorn and, but for Stirling's intervention, his rival would have lost the points he gained for his second place in Portugal and therefore the Championship too. Hawthorn, beset with failing brakes, stalled his engine while lying second to Moss on his last lap. After he had received the flag Moss saw him pushing his car in a vain attempt to restart it. He slowed and advised his rival to make use of a slope at the side of the circuit. This worked and so enabled Hawthorn to finish in second place ahead of Stewart Lewis-Evans' Vanwall. After the race the officials were intent on disqualifying Hawthorn for a breach of the rules but Moss persuaded them that the incident took place off the circuit and therefore was clearly permissible. So Stirling Moss, the quintessentially British sportsman, won the case for Mike Hawthorn at the cost of a World Championship which would otherwise have been his!

Yet the truth is that half a dozen World Championships could not have added any further to the stature of Sir Stirling Moss in motor racing.

Stirling Moss winning the 1961 Monaco Grand Prix, in Rob Walker's Lotus-Climax. The first World Championship of the 1.5 litre formula.

B. G. Apps

At the approach of 1959 Moss realised that the future lay with mid-engined cars and he drove Rob Walker's Cooper-Climax at Monaco, leading the race until he was sidelined by a broken Colotti gearbox. Then he drove the pale green P25 B.R.M. of the British Racing Partnership in Formula One and an Aston Marin in events for sports cars. He won, with Jack Fairman, the Nurburgring 1000 kilometres race in a works Aston Martin DBR1. The Aston failed at Le Mans with valve trouble, and his clutch broke on the B.R.M. at Rheims, but Stirling gained second place in the British Grand Prix at Aintree, which was to remain B.R.M.s best ever result in a British Grand Prix. Then he went on to win the Portuguese and Italian Grands Prix in the Rob Walker's Cooper-Climax. Sadly the Cooper's Colotti gear box let him down once more in the United States Grand Prix, so that he was robbed of a World Championship again.

In 1960 Moss won the Cuban Grand Prix in a Tipo 61 "Birdcage" Maserati, the Monaco Grand Prix in a Cooper-Climax, and the United States Grand Prix in Lotus-Climax.

Staying with Rob Walker in 1961, Moss won the Monaco Grand Prix after a heroic struggle, driving the Lotus-Climax on the limit throughout the race to hold off the more powerful shark-nosed Ferraris of Ritchie Ginther, Phil Hill and Wolfgang von Trips, and he beat the Italian cars again at the Nurburgring. It was another great race.

In 1986 I sent Rob Walker a painting of Stirling winning the Monaco Grand Prix in 1961, a race I had watched in the Students' Union at Oxford. He replied:

> "Thank you so very, very much for your lovely picture painting of Stirling Moss winning the Monaco G.P. in 1961 in the Lotus Climax 18. I am absolutely enchanted with it and have put it on the wall in my study next to the original painting of the same race by Michael Turner and they complement each other very well.
>
> I think that it was pure coincidence that Maurice Trintignant had the same number when he won for me in 1958 and in those days they only used the even numbers for the cars and our position after the works cars was usually about 10th so we got number 20 but in fact in the 1960 G.P. which Stirling won for me his number was 22.
>
> Thank you again for sending me the picture which I shall treasure and do keep in touch if you would like to do so."

He was kind to compare my very different view of the race to the well known painting of Michael Turner who is, of course, one of our great contemporary motor racing artists.

Although I never met Rob Walker his grandson told me that he had often seen my paintings in his study.

B. G. Apps '88

Stirling Moss winning the Brussels Grand Prix in Rob Walker's Lotus, in 1962.

For 1962 Moss was to have driven a dark blue shark-nosed Ferrari loaned to Rob Walker for the season, but sadly he crashed at Goodwood on Easter Monday in a pale green Cooper. Badly injured, he mercifully survived but, because he couldn't recall the incident or be sure of what caused it, he decided to retire from racing.

It so happened that Kath and I were married in St Peter's Church Carmarthen on that fateful Easter Monday in 1962. It was the only Easter Goodwood Meeting I had neither watched in person or seen on television, and I only heard the news of Stirling's crash the next morning in the County Hotel in Taunton when I read the headlines of the daily paper. It dominated our thoughts over a breakfast of kippers and, writing to me in 1985, Stirling said:

> *"It seems that that Easter Monday was quite a red letter day for both of us! I am glad to say that I am fully recovered. Not too wonderful in the memory department, but that may be attributable to age, rather than the bang on the head, However the latter provides a marvellous excuse!"*

In 1986 Stirling drove an Aston Martin DBR2 in the United States winning the main event but coming second to an *"extremely fast Chevrolet"* in a lesser event. I suggested that there should be a rule in motor racing that Chevrolets should not be allowed to overtake Aston Martins and that no one should be allowed to overtake Stirling Moss. He replied that Susie was with me regarding my suggested rules but that he wasn't sure how the Chevy drivers were going to feel about it!

In July 1994, after the tragic death of Senna, he wrote:

> *"It certainly was a terrible loss when Ayrton was killed. It is made even more tragic when you think how great he was and the fact that it was probably a mechanical failure and not an error on his part."*

Mercedes Benz was not always infallible and Stirling wrote to me about the disastrous 1955 Monaco Grand Prix.

> *"The race itself was a most depressing one for me because I really thought that I had won. Fangio was out with desmodroic valve problems and I was leading with only about fifteen laps to go (I think). And bang, Fangio's problem became mine too.*
> *I guess it was made far worse because Monaco is such an important event and I was still pretty young."*

He ended with, *"Roll on Goodwood and memories of the old days."*

Stirling was referring to the "Goodwood Revival" of Lord March. He will always be the star attraction at Goodwood where he is no less important than any of the cars.

MIKE HAWTHORN

MIKE HAWTHORN first came to the attention of close observers of the Sport when he raced a Riley Sprite with distinction, winning the Leinster Trophy in Wicklow and the Brooklands Memorial Trophy in 1951. George Abecassis invited him to drive an H.W.M. but he declined and, instead, Bob Chase bought a Cooper Bristol for him to drive and for his father Leslie to prepare. Leslie had raced motorcycles before the war and he and his son helped to complete the Cooper at the Surbiton works in time for it to arrive unpainted for the Easter Monday Goodwood meeting in 1952. This was the meeting at which the works cars of Eric Brandon and Alan Brown made their debut. Hawthorn's car ran on a mixture of fuel containing nitro methane, something that was kept a close secret from competitors, and it sported an extended air scoop over the bonnet designed to keep the opposition guessing! I was there to watch Mike Hawthorn sensationally draw away from the field to win the Chichester Cup convincingly. He wore what became his trade mark bow tie and removed his helmet on his victory lap to reveal a mop of blond hair, His six-foot-two frame sat tall in the car. He was second to the 4.5-litre "Thinwall Special" driven by Froilan Gonzales in the Richmond Trophy and ahead of Duncan Hamilton's beautiful old Lago Talbot.

Although he was very fast and competitive behind the wheel, Mike Hawthorn had a free and easy attitude to motor racing. At Turnberry in Scotland, where he was to drive the "Thinwall Special" he saw that Tony Rudd was holding things up on the starting grid because of a split fuel pipe on Parnell's B.R.M. The rather officious starter was insistent that the race should go ahead without the B.R.M., so Mike Hawthorn got out his car, strolled across to Tony Rudd and nonchalantly remarked that they couldn't start the race without them!

That year Mike Hawthorn finished third in the British, and fourth in the Belgian and Dutch Grands Prix with his Cooper Bristol and impressed Enzo Ferrari so much that he was offered a place in the works Ferrari team in 1953.

The green Ferrari

As a special concession to his young British driver Enzo Ferrari had his car painted green for the Argentine Grand Prix but Hawthorn was disappointed at finding that Alberto Ascari, Giuseppe Farina and Luigi Villoresi drew steadily away from him in their works cars. He finished fourth in an appalling race during which fifteen spectators were killed after one of them had run across the track in front of Farina's Ferrari. Two more were killed when they were mown down by an ambulance racing to the scene.

Mike bought a dark green jacket to compensate for the fact that his Ferrari was painted red after this. His finest race in 1953, and one of the greatest races of all time, was the French Grand Prix at Rheims. He was back in seventh place on a starting grid in which no less than ten Ferraris and Maseratis filled the first ten places. Yet Hawthorn won by one second after racing side by side with Fangio's Maserati A6SSG for lap after lap, the two finding time to smile at each other on the long straight.

Mike Hawthorn (16) and Juan Fangio (18), side-by-side, in the 1953 French Grand Prix.

Gregor Grant wrote in *Autosport* at the time, *"Everyone was on his (or her) feet. 'C'est Howtorn – non, c'est Fangio' howled the PA announcer. Up in the press tribunes the Argentinian commentator was practically in a state of collapse. He'd been jabbering away for over two and a half hours and could scarcely obtain any breathing space. Hard-headed journalists threw nonchalance to the winds. One gentleman even went so far as to tear up his notes, stand on his hat and finally fall over his desk."*

Chris Nixon in his superb book *Mon Ami Mate* records that Hawthorn was even able to read the Maserati's rev counter as they sped down the straight at maximum revs! It was deservedly described in the press as the "race of the century". Nixon also recalled that in the *Autosport* magazine Hawthorn said some years later of that race, *"Today I can admit that I was scared that the master was going to get very angry with such a newcomer, particularly in a World Championship event. Yet gradually I saw that he too was thoroughly enjoying himself, and as we went down the straight from Garenne, practically wheel-to-wheel, I would catch his infectious grin, which did more than anything else to give me the confidence I needed to keep up."*

Mike Hawthorn was also fourth in Holland, fifth in Britain, third in Switzerland and fourth in Italy, finishing fourth in the World Championship.

The Ferraris were no match for the new W196 Mercedes Benz in 1954 and the new pregnant-looking Super Squalo cars were outclassed. Hawthorn was injured in a crash at Syracuse but finished fourth in Belgium, second in Britain and Italy, and he won the Spanish Grand Prix which witnessed the promising debut of the Lancia D50 in the hands of Ascari and Villoresi. He finished third in the World Championship.

In 1955 Hawthorn drove for Tony Vandervell in Formula One and for Jaguar in sports car races. It was the year of the tragic accident at Le Mans. Hawthorn and Fangio had been re-enacting their 1953 Rheims duel, this time driving a Jaguar and a Mercedes, but as Hawthorn turned sharply into his pit at some speed, Lance Macklin was forced to take avoiding action in his Austin Healey. Pierre Levegh lost control of his Mercedes after striking the Austin Healey and crashed into the crowd with the loss of eighty lives. Hawthorn won the race for Jaguar after the Mercedes team withdrew, and he later won the Sebring 12 Hour race in the United States. He was to have joined the Lancia team but then the Lancia's were handed over to Enzo Ferrari lock stock and barrel.

In 1956 Hawthorn drove the new and fast P25 B.R.M. but the car proved to be unreliable and at times lethal, so he returned to Ferrari in 1957 to drive the Lancia Ferrari.

Hawthorn winning the French Grand Prix in 1958.

He and Peter Collins were both team mates and good friends at Ferrari and Roy Salvadori is reported to have said that this was not good for their team as neither was prepared to push the other hard to fight for position. Mike finished fourth in the French Grand Prix, third in the European Grand Prix at Aintree, second in the Italian Grand Prix and fourth in the World Championship.

Tragically Peter Collins was killed when his car left the track at speed and crashed during the German Grand Prix in 1958. Another of Hawthorn's team mates Luigi Musso was killed in the French Grand Prix that year. Driving the new V6 Ferrari Dino 246, Hawthorn won the French Grand Prix, and was second in Belgium, Britain, Portugal, Italy and Morocco. His team mate, Phil Hill, slowed to enable him to overtake to gain second place at Casablanca. It was sufficient for him to become Britain's first World Champion by one point from Stirling Moss. Stuart Lewis-Evans had been badly burned after his Vanwall's engine blew up during the Moroccan Grand Prix, and to the great distress of everyone, and in particular of Tony Vandervell who had never previously lost one of his drivers, Lewis-Evans died six days later.

Enzo Ferrari was determined to persuade Mike Hawthorn to drive for him in 1959 and he told his British driver that he could write his own contract which he would sign without reading. But Hawthorn had decided to retire from racing. With the death of his friend Peter Collins the fun had gone out of motor racing for him.

In addition to having the distinction of being the first British World Champion racing driver, Hawthorn also finished third in the Targa Florio and second in the Nurburgring 1000 kms.

Ironically in January 1959 Mike Hawthorn was killed when his 3.4-litre Jaguar crashed at speed on the Guildford bypass soon after overtaking Rob Walker's 300SL Mercedes Benz. It was raining, there were strong side winds, and he was possibly using an experimental hand throttle device in his car. It has also been said that he had a detestation of German cars and that, because of this, might have been attempting to prove a point in streaking away from the Mercedes. It emerged after his death that he was suffering with an incurable kidney condition and would have had less than two years to live.

TONY BROOKS

TONY BROOKS was studying dentistry when he first embarked upon his career in motor racing. He had competed in events with a Healey Silverstone, a DKW and a Fraser Nash before being invited to drive a privately-owned A-Type Connaught in a race at Crystal Palace in 1955. He finished in fourth place with only Hawthorn, Schell and Salvadori ahead of him in Formula One cars. Having a modest disposition and a reluctance to stand in the limelight, he always left it to his driving skill to do the talking for him and it spoke eloquently of his outstanding talent. Impressed by his performance in the early Connaught John Wyer invited Brooks to drive an Aston Martin DB3S in the 1955 Goodwood Nine Hours Race with Peter Collins and they finished in third place. This was followed by a second place at Aintree in another Connaught, and this in turn led Rodney Clark to invite him to drive the latest B-Type works car in the Syracuse Grand Prix in 1955. An account of this race appears earlier and it is sufficient here to record that Brooks surprised Musso and Villoresi in their works Maserati and everyone else by becoming the first British driver in a British car to win a Grand Prix since 1924. He had to be persuaded afterwards to join in the victory celebrations.

B.R.M. invited Tony to join Mike Hawthorn in driving the new P25 cars in 1956 and Brooks led the Aintree International 200 Miles Race comfortably until his disc brakes began to fade and

Tony Brooks driving the P25 B.R.M. in the Aintree International 200 miles race, in 1956.

Brooks and Fangio in the 1957 Italian Grand Prix.

Tony Brooks in Vanwall, numbered 28, at the start of the 1958 Italian Grand Prix at Monza.

he had to be content with second place. Both Brooks and Hawthorn had narrow escapes it the 2.5-litre B.R.Ms, with Brook's car overturning and being destroyed by fire during the British Grand Prix at Silverstone. Fortunately as there were no seat belts in those days he was thrown out and escaped serious injury.

B.G.Apps '07

Tony Brooks' Ferrari Dino 256, winning the German Grand Prix in 1959.

Understandably Tony Brooks left B.R.M. for Vanwall in 1957 and finished second in the Monaco Grand Prix and later in the season, suffering from his Le Mans injuries, he handed his car over to Stirling Moss during the British Grand Prix for him to go on and win it. Brooks later won the 1000 kilometre race at the Nurburgring for Aston Martin.

Still with Vanwall the next year, Brooks won the German, Belgian and Italian Grands Prix. Hawthorn won the World Championship with his Ferrari as Brooks and Moss had divided the ones he had failed to win between them.

In 1959 Brooks joined Ferrari to drive the last of their magnificent front-engined cars and he won the French and German Grands Prix, coming second in the World Championship to Jack Brabham's mid-engined Cooper.

After a season with the Yeoman Credit Team, Brooks went back to B.R.M. in 1960 but it was a disappointing stop gap year for B.R.M. as their Championship winning V8 car was not yet ready and he decided to retire at the end of the season.

Writing about the P25 B.R.M. which he drove in 1956 Tony Brooks told me:

"It was a very quick car, but unfortunately its road holding was rather poor to say the least and if I remember correctly the problem at Aintree was the not uncommon one of overheating and greatly reduced efficiency of the brakes due to the single disc at the rear operating on the transmission.

The B.R.M. flattered only to deceive on many occasions. It is a source of some regret that the car which won the World Drivers' Championship in 1962 was the one which should have been available at Monaco in 1961 but appeared for the first time in practice only at the Italian Grand Prix that year.

My last race before retirement was in the B.R.M. in the U.S. Grand Prix at Watkins Glen that year when it finished third, the best World Championship Grand Prix result the team had all season."

In 1992 I wrote to him about his contribution to the television series "The Power and the Glory" and asked him which of the cars he raced had given him most satisfaction.

Tony Brooks in his B.R.M. 572, at Monaco in 1961.

He wrote:

"I appeared in three of the thirteen episodes and I am sorry that you only happened to see the one where I was complaining about having to put on wet clothes at 3a.m. in the morning at Le Mans.

The various personal extracts were taken from a long interview and unfortunately, being out of context, they do not always convey the whole of what was intended.

The discomfort of wet clothing was only a minor part of my dislike of Le Mans which is not a race but rather a high speed tour with, in those days, a mix of cars with significant differences in performance. On the long straight in the misty, wet hours of darkness there could be as much as 100 miles per hour speed differential between one's car and those being overtaken.

The Connaught handled extremely well and I enjoyed myself at Syracuse. However, the 1959 Ferrari probably gave the greatest satisfaction in that each successive year produced better models and the Ferrari was the last of the front engined cars, which gave much more satisfaction than the rear engined ones, and it had a beautiful gearbox. The Vanwall was a difficult car to drive and therefore I also derived considerable satisfaction from the wins at the classic circuits of Spa, Nurburgring and Monza in 1958.

Later that year I met Tony Brooks with Kath and Michael for coffee at his garage in Weybridge near the old Brooklands motor racing circuit. He described motor racing in the 90s as being like mountaineering with a safety net. He welcomed the safer conditions but said that it was different and drivers would take fewer chances if each crash was likely to be their last – on tree-lined circuits. He also said that carbon fibre brakes might be banned so that the faster drivers could overtake on braking.

Tony Brooks was one of the really great motor racing drivers of all time and I am proud to be able to regard him as a friend. Kath and I greatly appreciate the card that we receive from Tony and Pina each Christmas.

JOHN SURTEES

GEOFF DUKE turned from motorcycle racing to motor racing when he joined the Aston Martin team and drove a DB3 at Sebring and elsewhere. Mike Hailwood made the same move from two to four wheels when he joined Team Surtees. But John Surtees alone achieved the ultimate success of becoming the World Champion on both two wheels and four. It is a distinction that no one else is ever likely to repeat.

His father Jack was three times British Motorcycle Sidecar Champion, and John started out by building his own 500cc racing motorcycle based on a 500cc Vincent and called the "Grey Flash." He came second to Geoff Duke at Thruxton in 1951.

Then he bought a more powerful Manx Norton and was invited to join the Norton works team in 1952. When Norton was in decline four years later he transferred to MV Augusta and won the 500cc World Motor Cycling Championship in 1956, and both 350cc and 500cc World Championships in the following two years. He also won six Isle of Man TT races.

Having done everything in motorcycle racing, in 1959 he tried a Vanwall and an Aston Martin and made the move to motor racing the following year. Driving for Ken Tyrrell he came second to Jim Clark in a Formula 500 race at Goodwood.

Next Colin Chapman signed him for Lotus and he finished second to Jack Brabham's Cooper-Climax in the British Grand Prix at Silverstone, proving at this early stage that he could excel in motor racing as he had already done in motorcycle racing. He took pole position for the Portuguese Grand Prix and led comfortably until he was forced to retire with a split radiator after hitting a curb. He declined to partner Jim Clark at Lotus the following year because it would have caused Innes Ireland to have been displaced and, after a spell with the Yeoman Credit Team, he joined Lola and came second in the British and German Grands Prix in 1962.

In 1963 John Surtees joined Enzo Ferrari, who appreciated his mechanical knowledge and skills, and he helped to develop the Dino 156. He was highly respected at Ferrari and given the name "Big John". He won the German Grand Prix two years running and the all-important Italian Grand Prix in 1964. In that year he also came second in Zandvoort, Watkins Glen and Mexico City and third at Silverstone, winning the World Championship in Formula One, and enabling Ferrari to win the Constructors' World Championship too. Graham Hill was second to him and Jim Clark third in the drivers' championship.

In 1965 John had a serious accident driving a Lola in Canada when a wheel came off his car at speed. He suffered multiple injuries but amazingly returned to the track in three months to win the 1000 Kilometre Race at Monza with Mike Parkes. After winning the Belgian Grand Prix for Ferrari in 1966, he left the Italian team and won the Mexican Grand Prix in a Cooper-Maserati.

In 1967 he joined Honda and won the Italian Grand Prix that year by 0.2 seconds from Jack Brabham.

Joining B.R.M. next he finished third in the 1969 United States Grand Prix in the troubled P139 but, being a perfectionist, he decided to establish his own team with his own cars and

John Surtees, finishing fourth
in the 1965 Monaco Grand
Prix, in the Ferrari 158, after
running out of fuel.

produced the Ford Cosworth-engined Surtees. Mike Hailwood won the European Formula Two Championship for Team Surtees and exchanged the lead with three other cars in the Italian Grand Prix before finishing fourth in 1971. John won the Oulton Park Gold Cup in his Surtees TS7 also in 1971.

Like the great Tazio Nuvolari John Surtees had successfully made the transition from motorcycle racing to motor racing and it is appropriate that he should have followed this by giving demonstration runs with the pre-war Auto Unions and Mercedes Benz to entertain the crowds at Goodwood in more recent years.

In 1986 I sent a painting to John of him winning the 1966 Belgian Grand Prix in a Ferrari and by chance it arrived the day before his birthday.

I had referred to myself as a mere spectator and he replied that the term did not do justice to me or to the millions of others who had followed the sport and helped to create the motorcycle and motor racing scene.

He wrote: *"Perhaps both you and I have seen the best years of racing with circuits now having changed out of all recognition and are either totally lined by brick walls, or else with the people being removed hundreds of yards away. And then of course we also have television which at least allows me to keep a little in touch with what goes on. I think you will agree, however, that unless one has really been part of the scene and really been able to take in the noises, the smells and the general ambience of the race circuit, then one is poorer for it."*

In 2001 I sent him a further painting, this time when he finished second at Mexico City 1964, thereby winning the World Championship.

He wrote about his choice of car for the race.

"Yes, it was a difficult decision. The 12 cylinder was a faster car because its Lucas injection was better suited to the altitude but we had a question mark about its reliability and particularly its consumption of oil so I opted for the 8.

John Surtees winning the
Belgian Grand Prix in his
Ferrari Tipo 312, in 1966.

It is only in this day and age that one appreciates quite how fragile and dangerous the cars of the Sixties were. I don't think modern drivers appreciate the privilege they now enjoy with a modern Grand Prix car in the way of safety and standards of engineering.

The Mercedes cars never go to the September event at Goodwood and this year I am missing it because I am going to a kart race with my son. The Festival of Speed, which takes place on 6-8 July in the grounds of Goodwood House, is the place where you will see the past and the present and certainly a good assortment of Mercedes. That is the one to go to if you would like to browse around the cars. If you would like me to arrange something in the way of tickets for you I would be pleased to do it."

He was as good as his word and I went with Kath and Michael that July when we were delighted to have an opportunity to meet John and to have a chat with him.

SIR JACKIE STEWART

HAVING SENT paintings to Enzo Ferrari and Stirling Moss, I sent a third in 1985 to Jackie Stewart. It was of him driving the Tyrrell Ford in 1970 and he wrote:

I am glad to hear of your interest in Grand Prix racing – your reference to Goodwood in 1949 brings back to me memories because I still have the autograph book I was given in 1949, when I was 10, and in that book are some wonderful signatures of some of the great race drivers – Ascari, Fangio, Villoresi, Taruffi, Stirling Moss, Mike Hawthorn, etc. I dare say we were keen on the same business around the same time, and gladly both of us have the good fortune to be blessed with being able to enjoy the world of Motor Sport to this day. Long may it last!

Jackie Stewart started his sporting career with shooting and he won the British Grand Prix on two occasions as well as the English, Irish, Scottish and Welsh Championships. His interest in motor racing was due to his elder brother Jimmy, for whom his father bought a C-Type Jaguar for £1,800. Jimmy drove a Cooper Bristol for Ecurie Ecosse in the British Grand Prix in 1953 where his race ended abruptly at Copse Corner and Jackie, having access to the paddock, obtained the autographs of all the top drivers.

Following in Jimmy's footsteps, Jackie signed with Ecurie Ecosse in February 1963 and, as he records in his autobiography, *Winning is Not Enough*, Helen bought half a yard of Royal Stewart tartan silk to stick around his white helmet with nail varnish. It became his trademark.

Jimmy Clark was a close friend and advised him that the best man to drive for was Ken Tyrrell, and Ken, having been impressed when he saw Jackie during a test in a Formula Three Cooper lap faster than Bruce McLaren, invited him to drive his Cooper in Formula Three in 1964. His first win was at Snetterton and he went on to win the Formula Three Championship for Tyrrell that year.

This success led to Jackie being offered places in the Formula One teams of Cooper, Lotus and B.R.M. He chose B.R.M. and wrote the following about it to me about it only recently. *"When I joined B.R.M. in 1965 it was my entry into Formula One as a works driver; a very big moment in my life and my career. The Team Manager was Tony Rudd, a very able man, Graham Hill was to be my team mate, Raymond Mays was still around, and at that time, although perhaps not as fast as the Lotus, the B.R.M. was the most robust. I was lucky enough to win a non-Championship Formula One race at the Daily Express International Trophy race at Silverstone, followed by the Italian Grand Prix later in the season, while finishing second three times to Jim Clark at the Belgian, French and Dutch Grands Prix. I finished third in the World Championship that year, driving the very strong, robust and reliable B.R.M."*

Writing to me in July 2003, Tony Rudd spoke about the B.R.M. that Jackie Stewart drove that year. *"I felt the 261 monocoques were better than the opposition – Italian GP at Monza – and the best cars B.R.M. had built."* Jackie Stewart and Graham Hill had of course finished first and second at Monza in that order.

Jackie Stewart with B.R.M. in 1965.

In 1966 Stewart was leading the Indianapolis 500 race in a Lola when his car broke down only eight laps from the end. Then at Spa he was trapped in his wrecked car having come off the circuit at high speed in the rain. Graham Hill and Bob Bondurant also crashed at about the same spot and came over to help him. Drenched with highly inflammable fuel in a car that could have exploded at any moment as the electrics could not be switched off, he was trapped by the steering wheel which could only be removed by a spanner. Graham stayed with him while Bob ran across the track to ask if anyone in the crowd had a spanner. One was found in the boot of a spectator's car and so the steering wheel was removed. An ambulance only arrived later and Louis Stanley accompanied Jackie to hospital. In *Winning is Not Enough* Jackie recalls that he addressed Louis Stanley as "Lewis" several times before being told *"Stewart, if you insist upon calling me by my first name, it is Louis, not Lewis."* That was typical of Louis Stanley. The ambulance driver lost his way in driving to the hospital and Louis Stanley and Jackie decided to launch a campaign to provide better medical facilities at the circuits. The result was a mobile operating theatre equipped to provide the highest quality of treatment immediately at the circuits. Jackie also became President of the Grand Prix Drivers' Association and led the campaign to have Armco safety barriers for circuits, flame proof overalls and officially certified helmets for drivers, and six point safety harnesses. He and the G.P.D.A. caused the German Grand Prix to be switched from the Nurburgring to Hockenheim on safety grounds.

Jackie had to contend with a good deal of criticism for his campaign to make motor racing safer but it was necessary. He recalled that he had lost fifty-seven friends and colleagues in only eleven years and, amongst those his three closest friends, Jimmy Clark, Jochen Rindt and Francois Cevert.

B.R.M. produced an H16 engine for the 3-litre Formula and I hoped that it would possess something like the potential of the original V16 and, at the same time, prove to be reliable. Sadly that was not the case and Jackie ruefully records that it used too much fuel, oil and water and was chronically unreliable. Jim Clark scored the engine's only win and that was in a Lotus.

As a result of this Jackie turned to Ken Tyrrell again but this time to drive in Formula One. He drove Tyrrell's Ford Cosworth-engined Matra in 1968 and won the Dutch, French, British, and United States Grands Prix, coming second in the Drivers' World Championship. The next year

Jackie Stewart with his Tyrrell-Ford at Watkins Glen in 1970.

he won his first World Championship with the Matra, winning in South Africa, Spain, Holland, France, Britain and Italy.

In 1970 Matra insisted that Ken Tyrrell should use the new V12 Matra engines and, unimpressed with them, he decided to buy a Cosworth-engined March instead. He won the Spanish Grand Prix and came second at Zandvoort and Monza but neither Ken nor Jackie were happy with the car, and Ken decided to build his own car instead in the woodshed of his headquarters in Ockham where he and his family had been timber merchants. It is impossible to imagine anything like this happening today. He commissioned Derek Gardner, who had previously been with Ferguson working on four wheel drive cars, to design the car in utter secrecy. According to Doug Nye in *Famous Racing Cars* Ken told him that, for reasons of sponsorship, it had to be ready for the Gold Cup at Oulton Park that year or *"you might as well chuck it in the Thames"*. The car was 100 lbs lighter than the March and had a low bulbous monocoque body. It cost Ken £22,500 minus engine and gearbox and this compared with £9,000 for a March. With the help of Walter Hassan of Ford, ELF fuel and Goodyear tyres it duly appeared at Oulton Park where Jackie Stewart broke the lap record before retiring. In 1971 Jackie won the World Championship with the new car, winning no less than six of the eleven World Championship events and gaining almost twice as many points as Ronnie Peterson who came second with a March Ford and a March Alfa Romeo. Jackie's team mate Francois Cevert came third after winning the United States Grand Prix and finishing third in France and Germany.

1972 was Emerson Fittipaldi's year with his JPS Lotus Ford but Jackie won four Grands Prix and came second in the World Championship and Francois Cevert sixth. Then 1973 brought a third Championship for Jackie and Tyrrell with five wins and two second places.

Jackie decided that he would retire at the end of the season. It proved to be a tragic end because during practice for the United States Grand Prix at Watkins Glen Francois Cevert struck the guard rail while driving through the Esses at high speed. The car shot across the track into the

Jackie Stewart with his Tyrrell-Ford at Monaco in 1973.

Signed painting of Jackie Stewart winning the German Grand Prix in 1973, in his Tyrrell-Ford.

opposite barrier and Cevert was killed instantly. Jackie Stewart withdrew from the race and announced his retirement. Both he and Ken were devastated by the loss of this handsome and charismatic young Frenchman and Ken always maintained afterwards that he would have been a brilliant World Champion had he lived.

Jackie Stewart was presented with Tyrrell 003 as a retirement gift and although Ken continued to develop and race Tyrrell cars for many more years he never again achieved the success he had enjoyed with Jackie Stewart.

With his son Paul, Jackie later established the Stewart Formula One Team and Johnny Herbert won the European Grand Prix at the Nurburgring in the Stewart Ford in 1999. The team was eventually bought by Jaguar and then by Red Bull. When I met Paul after the funeral of Ken Tyrrell he reminded me that Stewart Fords had in different World Championship events managed first, second and third places.

When Jackie was granted a knighthood in 2001 for his outstanding achievements in Formula One he chose as his motto "Integrity and Care." That summed up his approach to motor racing and the reason why he entitled his book *Winning is Not Enough*.

Speaking at Beaulieu in 2008 Jackie said that his technique had been to "drive slow enough to win but fast enough to stay ahead." At the Nurburgring his car would take off thirteen times each 14.7 mile lap of the race but he said that liberties could be taken with cars today that were not possible in his day. He said that the problem today was that brakes were too efficient leaving too little room in approaching a corner for the faster drivers to overtake and that less down force would make overtaking more possible. Jackie also thought that there should be penalties to discourage drivers from leaving the circuit. I was particularly interested to hear Sir Jackie say that the finest, and the most perfectly balanced car that he had ever driven was the Type 31 Alfa Romeo which Tazio Nuvolari drove in the 1930s.

JAMES HUNT

JAMES HUNT was larger than life. The son of Wallis Hunt, a stock broker, he was educated at Wellington College and excelled at tennis, cross country and squash. He was charming, handsome, charismatic and flamboyant. He would arrive at formal occasions barefoot and in jeans and became a national figure through his high profile life style and his successes in Formula One.

He first became interested in motor racing when he watched his elder brother racing a Mini at Silverstone and, although it was intended that he should study medicine, he stacked shelves in a supermarket to raise the funds to buy a Mini for himself. Early on in his career he became known as "Hunt the Shunt" because, although he was extremely fast he was also prone to accidents. He claimed that most of his shunts were multiple ones, implying that they were not directly his fault. On the other hand he was honest and inclined to understate his racing skills, reminiscent of drivers in an earlier age.

In 1971 Hunt was invited by the March Team to race in both Formula Three and Formula Two and then he joined Lord Alexander Hesketh and Anthony "Bubbles" Horsley to drive for the Hesketh team. He wrote off a Formula Two Surtees while testing it and, having had little success in the lower formulae. Lord Hesketh calculated that it would only cost one-third more to compete in Formula One. He purchased a March 731 which was developed by Dr Harvey Postlethwaite and James came second with it in the United States Grand Prix at Watkins Glen, third in the Dutch Grand Prix at Zandvoort and seventh in the 1973 World Championship.

Speaking in *Champion Hunt*, in Duke's "Profile of a Legend" Series, James said that the Hesketh Team's approach to racing was novel as the workers stuck to their tasks while Alexander's friends were *"keen and committed Partiers"* with vodka's from ten in the morning. The set up was very much in the tradition of the Bentley Boys at Brooklands and, with their Hesketh cars painted patriotically in red white and blue and James Hunt as their driver, they achieved wonders against their commercially financed rivals.

In his book *James Hunt: Against the Odds*, Eoin Young writes that he had a disregard for convention. He himself said, "Its really the principle of the thing, to do what I want to do whenever I can. Life is too short to be bound by regulations when it isn't absolutely essential." But Young wrote that he was something of a prisoner of his own reputation and James revealed that he was not a hard drinker. *"I don't like champagne, and especially not after a race. I prefer a beer to quench my thirst and I'll take wine with a meal from time to time."*

The Hesketh 308, designed by Postlethwaite with a monocoque construction, Ford Cosworth engine and Hewland gearbox, was unveiled at the beginning of 1974. A V12 Hesketh engine was proposed but never built. James gained third places in the Swedish, Austrian and United States Grands Prix and finished eighth in the World Championship while Hesketh was fourth in the Constructor's Championship.

The following year James won his first Formula One Grand Prix with the Hesketh at Zandvoort and finished fourth in the World Championship.

After the race James said, *"Crossing the line first at Zandvoort improved my driving more than anything else. It rounded off my education, and I felt I could get on top of the others. When they are sitting behind you then you can jolly well dictate your way of doing things."*

In 1975 the Hesketh 308C appeared with Aeon suspension. Hunt won his first Formula One Grand Prix with the new Hesketh at Zandvoort. He was second at Buenos Aires and Paul Ricard and both he and Hesketh finished fourth in the World Championships, Niki Lauda and Ferrari winning them both.

It was said that Lord Hesketh was reluctant to accept a major sponsor for the team and so withdrew from the Formula One scene after providing a colourful and entertaining episode in motor racing for all the British enthusiasts.

Lord Hesketh, in response to a painting I had sent him wrote, *"Thank you very much for your charming painting which has given me enormous pleasure even if it is accompanied with a whiff of nostalgia. It is always very rewarding to discover that Hesketh Racing is not entirely forgotten."*

From Hesketh James Hunt turned to McLaren and was given the seat vacated by Emerson Fittipaldi, who had moved to the Copersucar team, and won the Spanish, French, German, Dutch, Canadian, and United States Grands Prix, and the World Championship by one point from Niki Lauda, after the Austrian had withdrawn from the Japanese Grand Prix because of the torrential rain.

The new McLaren M26 was beset with mechanical problems in 1977 but still James won four Grands Prix and finished fifth in the World Championship.

He left McLaren in 1979 to move to the Wolfe Team but retired from racing after the Monaco Grand Prix the following year.

In *James Hunt: Against the Odds* Hunt's words about his relationship with his great rival Niki Lauda reflect a level of sportsmanship that has not always been apparent since. *"He'll make himself as tough as he can to be overtaken in an absolutely fair way, but the moment you're alongside or if*

Lord Hesketh with James Hunt, driving the Formula One Hesketh.

James Hunt winning the
British Grand Prix at Brands
Hatch in 1976, with his
McLaren Ford.

you've got the line, he won't start doing anything silly which is very important. It means that we always have a clean race together."

When he retired James joined Murray Walker at B.B.C. television and they formed a brilliant partnership in providing a commentary on all the Formula One events, and James could be brutally outspoken in his assessment of the drivers.

Writing to me in 1986 James said, "I am glad that you enjoy the television coverage of Grand Prix racing. It is nice for me to be able to continue my involvement with the sport (in comparative safety) and rewarding to know that so many people are interested in the coverage."

In spite of being called Hunt the Shunt, James was as aware as anyone of the real dangers of motor racing in his day. Writing in 1977 he said, "The danger aspect is the biggest cloud on my horizon, and a constant heavy thought at home – its not something to think about in the emotionally charged atmosphere at a circuit. One has to weigh the odds, the risks involved, as well as you can and look at life and see if it is worth taking the risk for the time being."

He was with Murray and the B.B.C. for thirteen years but died of a heart attack at the age of forty-five in his home.

NIGEL MANSELL

NIGEL MANSELL put the fun back into Formula One for seasoned followers of the sport and also created a whole new generation of enthusiasts for whom his name became synonymous with motor racing. "Mansell Mania" gripped the nation and especially the crowds who cheered him on to victory

Motor racing began for Nigel with Formula Ford and he won the Formula Ford Championship in 1977. He and Rosanne made great sacrifices, selling their home and their car, in order to obtain a seat for him in a Formula Three March to further his career. Following a serious accident he was told that he would never be able to drive again but he defied the doctor's orders with typical grit and determination, accepting an invitation to test a Formula One Lotus. In spite of a severely injured back, his potential was obvious to Colin Chapman who signed him as a test driver in 1979. He partnered Elio de Angelis in the JPS Lotus Formula One Team in 1981.

Sadly Colin Chapman died suddenly the following year and Nigel left Lotus at the end of 1984. Frank Williams then invited him to drive a Williams Honda as Keke Rosberg's team mate and he won his first Grand Prix at Brands Hatch in 1985.

The following year Nigel was the team mate of World Champion Nelson Piquet and, in a letter to Frank Williams, I pointed out how wonderful it would be if a British driver was to win the World Championship in one of his cars.

Nigel Mansell winning the British Grand Prix at Brands Hatch in 1985.

Signed photograph of Nigel
Mansell in 1986.

Frank Williams replied, *"Thank you for your good wishes for this season and of course we will certainly be doing our very best to win this year's Championship – with either Nelson Piquet (who has replaced Keke) or Nigel Mansell. A British driver winning the Championship would of course be excellent, but I don't think we'll complain too much if Nelson Piquet wins the Championship!"*

Soon afterwards Frank Williams had his devastating road accident which left his life hanging in the balance for a number of days. Nigel Mansell was testing at Paul Ricard at the time and, having rushed to the scene of the accident, went with Frank to the hospital.

I sent a painting to Nigel that March and he wrote:

> *"Your superb painting arrived at our home the other week, completely intact and undamaged. It now stands proudly in our lounge awaiting a suitable frame, so it can be hung on the wall. Unfortunately the first race of the season was very disappointing for me and, along with poor Frank's accident it hasn't been the best of starts to the season.*
>
> *However our thoughts and prayers are constantly with Frank, and I know things can only get better on the track, so we're going for a "championship" year."*

That April Bernie Ecclestone very generously sent me a Paddock Pass for the British Grand Prix at Brands Hatch saying that it would *"enable me to get a little closer to the heat of the action"*. Walking around the transporters in the Paddock before the race I came across Nigel Mansell, sitting in the back of a large Williams lorry with its tail gate down, so I was able to wish him good luck before finding the most suitable place from which to watch the start. At the start Nigel's car only crept forward from the front row and was soon overtaken by the entire field. He later said that something had exploded behind his back and it seemed that his race was over before it started. However, the Ligier of Jacque Laffitte became involved in a multiple pile up at Paddock Bend and the unfortunate French driver broke both his legs. It meant that the race had to be stopped and it could only be restarted after the helicopter that took the Ligier driver to Sidcup hospital had returned to be ready for any further incident. This allowed time for the spare Williams to be prepared for Nigel.

A hundred and fifty thousand people in addition to myself had come to watch Mansell win, and this time he got away to a very reasonable start as he familiarised himself with the spare Williams. He caught up to second place behind Piquet and was content to run a few lengths behind until lap 23 when he passed him to take the lead. Piquet pulled into the pits for new tyres on the 30th lap and two laps later Nigel came in for the same reason. He came back on to the track just ahead and, although disadvantaged by the poor grip of his cold tyres, Nigel succeeded in holding Piquet off, the two at one point running side by side, until his tyres were warm. Then Nigel drew steadily further ahead to win the race. The crowd went wild with excitement and it was an occasion not to be missed.

Signed painting of Nigel Mansell and his Williams Honda in 1986.

Nigel wrote to me afterwards saying that Nelson Piquet only missed one gear during the whole race and it cost him the lead.

With his famous Red Five Williams Honda, Nigel won five races and he would have won the World Championship in 1986 had it not been that one of his rear tyres burst at approaching 200mph in Adelaide. His car came to rest after snaking from side to side right in front of a television camera. It had required superlative skill to hold it all together, and I watched it at home in Bournemouth as it happened.

1987 would have been a successful year for Nigel had it not been for a crash during qualifying for the Japanese Grand Prix which meant that he had to miss the remaining events. The following year Williams lost their Honda turbocharged engine to McLaren and the normally aspirated Williams Judd was uncompetitive.

In 1989 Nigel was invited by Enzo Ferrari to drive his new John Barnard designed car and in a letter he wrote to me in January he said, *"Well, we are into the new year, new team and new car (plenty of pasta!). Your tremendous support is, as ever, much appreciated. Fingers crossed for a good season."*

Nigel won the Brazilian and Hungarian Grands Prix and gained the title "Il Leone" throughout Italy from grateful fans. However the Ferrari proved not to be a match for the Williams Renault. In September Nigel sent me a special limited edition signed print of his Ferrari by Benjamins *"to show my appreciation of your encouragement, support and of course, of the paintings which you have kindly sent to me over the years."*

The following year, after five wins in a row and nine in all, he won the World Championship.

I received a personal Christmas card from Nigel and Rosanne each year and this was always eagerly awaited. Every year, on the Sunday evening before Christmas, members of the Church Council came to the Vicarage with their husbands or wives to enjoy mulled wine and mince pies in front of a roaring open fire. Before long someone would be sure to ask, "Where is Nigel Mansell's Christmas card?" Then the card would be produced and passed around with great care and ceremony for everyone to examine and admire.

Nigel and Rosanne's 1992
Christmas card.

Nigel Mansell, World
Champion in 1983.

In 1999, quite unknown to me, Nigel very generously agreed to write a Foreword in the
programme of a concert by the Morriston Orpheus Choir to mark my 21 years at All Saints'
Church. He wrote *"Ours is a long-standing friendship and over many years we have corresponded
avidly. I have always taken a keen interest in, and much admired Bryan's skills as a motor sports enthusiast, and in this I am by no means alone."* I had always wanted to be a couple of inches taller and I
think I achieved it that evening!

In 1993 Nigel joined the Newman-Haas team to compete in the CART series in a Lola Ford.
The great rival of Newman Haas was Roger Penske whose cars were constructed only a few miles
away from me in Poole in Dorset. In 1992 Nick Goozee, the Managing Director of Penske Cars
offered to give me a tour of their premises, suggesting sometime between September and January
when they would have a complete car on the premises. I went in early November with my neighbour Brian Green and it so happened that I was wearing a clerical collar. Afterwards Nick wrote,
*"It was a pleasure to meet you both and to enjoy your genuine enthusiasm for the sport. There was much
speculation about your presence here at Penske, one wag being moved to enquire if the problems facing
us were bad enough for me to consider all resources!"* He invited me to watch Sky TV coverage of
the Indianapolis 500 Race on their big screen at the factory in 1993.

Nigel Mansell was the first Rookie to win his first race, at the Surfers' Paradise in Australia and he came close to winning the Indianapolis 500 Race, going on to become the first driver to win both the World Formula One Championship and the Indy Car Championship in successive years.

In 1994 he returned to Williams after the tragic death of Ayrton Senna and won the Australian Grand Prix. The next year he joined McLaren but, unhappy with the car, retired from Formula One after two races.

Roger Penske and the Penske team in 1992.

Nigel Mansell and the Newman-Haas Indy car.

B.G. Apps '94

Nigel Mansell winning the
Australian Grand Prix in 1994.

There was never a dull race when Nigel Mansell was involved. He was always fiercely competitive but fair, and never gave up. He would win against the odds when circumstances had placed him at a disadvantage. In his *Formula One Heroes* Murray Walker wrote, *"Nigel is an extraordinary mixture. In the cockpit he was inspired: gutsy, single-mindedly determined, awesomely brave and with an implacable will to win. He gave me more magic commentary moments than all the rest of them put together, because wherever he was there was drama and excitement."*

The Mansell years were good years for British motor racing and for me as his supporter and friend.

KEN TYRRELL

I N 1985 I innocently wrote to Ken Tyrrell to ask his advice about how to go about watching the Friday practice for the British Grand Prix at Silverstone. I was committed to conducting services on the Sunday but thought that the previous Friday would give me an opportunity to see the drivers and their cars in action. In my ignorance I thought that I might have arrived only to discover that the general public was not allowed in! I strongly suspect that Ken assumed it was a none too subtle attempt to gain a Paddock Pass, and I was astonished and delighted when he sent me one! He wrote:

> "With reference to your letter regarding the British Grand Prix at Silverstone, I am sure you will understand that our allocation of passes is strictly limited. Also, being the home Grand Prix, many of our staff wish to attend.
>
> Nevertheless, I am enclosing a pass that will admit you to the circuit, paddock and pits on Friday, July 19th.
>
> Please be sure to return the pass to me or one of my staff before you leave on Friday, so that it can be used by one of my staff on Saturday.
>
> I look forward to meeting you at Silverstone."

I set out from Bournemouth long before dawn and it was still very early when I arrived at Brackley. Having left in the dry I ran into torrential rain and had to park outside a shop in Brackley for three-quarters of an hour before it opened so that I could buy some protection from the weather!

In spite of this delay I still arrived at the circuit in very good time and found my way to the Tyrrell Pits where two or three mechanics were already standing around the dark blue cars. One, which was to be driven by Martin Brundle had a new Renault Turbo engine while the other, for Stefan Bellof, had the tried and tested Ford DVF. I had time to walk around the Ferrari, Lotus and McLaren Pits and, in particular, to photograph some of the drivers, including Aryton Senna. Eventually the Tyrrell drivers arrived and they both engaged Ken Tyrrell in serious conversation about the cars and the race as soon as he came in. Engines were fired up with a sound that was painful until I applied some earplugs, and there was also a strong smell of burning fuel as the engines were extended within the confines of the garages. I was fascinated to see how quickly the cars could be taken apart and reassembled, with wheels and engine covers being removed for adjustments to be made. Ken was a towering figure of authority and good humour, briefly welcoming me before crossing the pit lane to stand on the strip that separated the pit lane from the track itself to watch the cars as they passed by at speed. The cars frequently returned to the pits for attention by the mechanics and Ken would come back to have a further word with the drivers. The strict warning on the back of my paddock pass was that it would be instantly confiscated if the holder attempted to venture into the pit lane, but that didn't stop Ken from suggesting that I should go across with him to get better shots with my camera!

Ken Tyrrell in the Tyrrell pits,
at Silverstone.

The Turbo charged Alfa Romeos of Riccardo Patrese and Eddie Cheever which frequently
returned to the pit next door to Tyrrell pits, after blowing up in clouds of fire and smoke, enlivened
the proceedings! The Turbo engined Tyrrell was disappointing and neither Martin Brundle nor
Stefan Bellof could approach the lap times of Nigel Mansell's Williams. Sadly Bellof was killed
later that season in a sports car race and Ken told me that he was certain that, had he lived, he
would have had a great future in motor racing.

I sent Martin Brundle a painting of his car leaving the pits at Silverstone and he wrote, *"You have
got the proportions of the car just right. I am afraid it's a car which I have had a love-hate relationship
with. It hasn't been the best of cars to drive, frightening me silly on several occasions, but at the same time
it did get me to the finish line at many Grands Prix.*

*After only a handful of laps I get the feeling that our new car, the 015, will be much quicker, enabling
me to challenge regularly for top 3 placings."* I shared Martin's hope.

The following year I went to the Silverstone paddock thanks to Bernie Ecclestone but after
that Ken sent me a Paddock Pass each year until he sold the Tyrrell Team to B.A.R.

On many occasions I was accompanied by my neighbour Brian Green, who is a professional
artist, although naturally he was unable to enjoy the advantages of my Paddock Pass. In the earlier

Martin Brundle's Tyrrell in the pit lane at Silverstone in 1985.

The paddock pass given to me by Bernie Ecclestone.

Chris Barber with the Tyrrell team in 1994.

years I found that, being amongst the first to arrive, many of the officials at the various barriers were mystified by my pass. Once, when Douglas Eyre, who was later a Mayor of Bournemouth, was with me we were waved through so many check points that we began to wonder if we would end up on the circuit itself and began to retrace out steps!

As the years passed I noticed that security at Silverstone steadily increased while at the same time the facilities were improved. The teams introduced lavish motor homes and I would enjoy a mid morning coffee and midday lunch with Ken and Norah in the Tyrrell motor home. Ken was of course very well known and everyone regarded him with great affection and respect. He introduced me to many of the great names in motor racing, including Sir Jack Brabham. One year my fellow guest in the Tyrrell home was the famous band leader Chris Barber. He had promised to put on a concert in honour of Ken if the cars won another Grand Prix and there was some discussion as to what venue would be large enough to accommodate the audience. Ken showed him a portrait I had recently done of him and, when he said that he didn't have one of himself, I promised to send him one.

The glory days of Jackie Stewart had long passed but, as well as thoroughly enjoying motor racing, Ken was as serious as he had ever been in his approach to the sport. He invited me to the Tyrrell Factory in Ockham on one occasion and the scene reminded me of those scenes in James Bond films in which all kinds of new gadgets for the Secret Service are being put through their paces. In one corner an experiment was being carried out which involved the injection of oil into the machinery under pressure with the object of gaining a minute fraction of a second each lap. Designer Harvey Postlethwaite was often a step ahead of the game, as when he introduced an entirely new and revolutionary anhedral high nose. It was soon copied by all the other teams but for a while Tyrrell was able to exploit its advantage.

Underfunded in the later years, Tyrrell always did better at the beginning of each year as Ken lacked the resources to develop the cars as the other teams did during the course of each season

The United States Grand Prix in 1990 witnessed a glorious episode when Jean Alesi took the lead in his Tyrrell and held it for thirty laps. When Senna at last overtook him, Alesi briefly re-took the lead and eventually finished in a very fine second place.

In those days it was possible for me to approach the drivers as they sat in their cars in the pits area and Ayrton Senna signed a painting while waiting to drive down the pit lane for a practice session. He wrote to me briefly in February 1987 expressing confidence that it would be a good year for him.

A note from Ayrton Senna in February 1987.

Painting, signed by Ayrton Senna in his car before a practice sesson, of his win in Detroit, 1987, with the Lotus Honda.

When Ken first introduced me to Jean Alesi in the pits it was against the roar of the engines being warmed up in the pits. He shouted "This is Bryan – he is a priest" – putting his hands together as if in prayer – "he paints" – stroking the air with an imaginary brush – "and if you get on the right side of him he'll put a good word in for you with the Man up there" – pointing to the heavens. I'm not sure how much Jean Alesi got of that.

Once I told Ken that I had sent a painting to Eddie Jordan and he laughed down the phone and said "his team really needs your prayers!"

The Tyrrells were seriously underfunded over all those years and I suggested to Ken once that he should sign a top driver regardless of the cost and then, having achieved this advantage, secure a substantial sponsor to provide the funds. He told me that sadly it didn't work like that.

On one occasion his cars were called for a spot check at the beginning of practice and it meant that they missed the whole session. It was a routine procedure that could be imposed without warning on any team and I suggested that it would be much more reasonable if the cars were checked when the session was over. Ken roared with laughter and said, "How green can you get! If the teams had prior warning of it you could be sure that all the cars would comply with the rules at the time when they were inspected."

Over lunch one year I asked the wife of the Italian driver Stefano Modena how she coped with the element of danger in motor racing and instantly realised it was the wrong thing to say. Norah forestalled her answer by quickly saying, "We don't think about that."

Ken Tyrrell and Mark Blundell's Tyrell Yamaha 022.

In addition to being enthusiastic about football and cricket Ken enjoyed shooting for game. It was something we disagreed about but could discuss with good humour.

In February 1998 Ken wrote to me about the take over of Tyrrell by B.A.R.

Following the recent acquisition of the Tyrrell Racing Organisation by British American Racing, it had been the intention for us to stay with the company until the end of the year, but after a great deal of thought we have decided to step back now.

My last 30 years (and Bob's 24 years) in Formula One have provided us with the most challenging and rewarding times, many of which we have been pleased to share with you.

Tyrrell's challenge for the 1998 season will be led by Harvey Postlethewaite, supported by Rupert Manwaring Commercial Director, Mike Gascoyne Deputy Technical Director and Steve Nielsen Team Manager.

We wish Tyrrell and British American Racing every success.

I wrote to Ken asking if he could send me some small souvenir of no intrinsic value which I could keep, and I happened to mention that as a small boy I had removed a cigarette stubber from a bus as a souvenir, thinking that this alone would be preserved for posterity after the bus was eventually scrapped. The theft weighed heavily on my conscience for many years.

Ken replied:

All good things come to an end but this good thing did end rather abruptly. I have arranged for something suitable as a souvenir to be sent to you and now it is my turn to have a guilty conscience as the item being sent to you is really the property of B.A.R, if this makes you a receiver of stolen property I apologise.

I have enjoyed knowing you over the years and hope we shall meet again.

N. A. Davis, the Factory Manager posted the souvenir.

Ken has passed your recent letter over to me to answer and to find a keepsake from one of the best of the Tyrrell cars before we become history.

I thought you might like this front stub axle and wheel nut from an 025 car, you can screw the nut on and off and probably imagine all sorts of things from wheel changes to pit stop mishaps!

Ken has asked me to pass on his and Norah's best wishes.

Sadly B.A.R.'s main purpose in acquiring Tyrrell was to gain its revenue from T.V. as an established Formula One team. No further cars were produced at Ockham and the highly talented staff disbursed to other teams.

Harvey Postlethwaite very kindly wrote to me before the next British Grand Prix to offer me a Paddock Pass but this was just before my heart bypass operation and so I had very reluctantly to decline. All the same a Pass did arrive with a note which read *"Please find enclosed your pass for Friday at the British Grand Prix – please ensure that you return it to either Steve Nielsen or Kate Aspinall of the Tyrrell Team prior to leaving the Paddock on Friday afternoon."* I had to return it regretfully with thanks.

After the race Harvey Postlethwaite moved to Toyotta to design their first Grand Prix contender but sadly died of a heart attack soon afterwards.

Kath and I called on Ken and Norah in their beautiful old Rectory in West Clandon and had lunch with them on a number of occasions afterwards and, on one such occasion, he was interested to study my albums of pictures and correspondence at some length, making frequent comments about the racing drivers or others who had written to me. He brought downstairs a large scale model of the six wheel P34 Tyrrell in a glass case which ELF had presented to him. Sadly Ken was receiving chemotherapy and died not long afterwards. Norah was also unwell and all too soon she too had passed on. Their son Ken phoned to thank me for being a good friend to them both but it had been a privilege, and the pleasure was all mine. May they rest in peace.

Ken and Norah Tyrrell in the Tyrrell motor home at Silverstone in 1995.

Michele Alboreto's Ferrari in the pit lane, Silverstone, 1985.

Mansell pursuing Piquet at Brands Hatch in 1986.

Nigel Mansell's Williams-Honda in the Silverstone pit lane in 1987.

Ayrton Senna's Lotus Honda in the pit lane, at Silverstone in 1987.

Mark Blundell in the Tyrrell pit in 1994.

Mechanics tending Damon Hill's Williams Renault in 1994.

WHEN DID MOTOR RACING STOP BEING FUN?

W E MIGHT have no problem identifying a period in motor racing when the sport was fun for drivers and spectators alike, but it is not so easy to pinpoint a moment in time when this ceased to be the case, if indeed it ever did.

We can talk about the good old days, when racing cars looked like cars, and when anyone who drove a family saloon could relate to the controls of a racing car, but does the argument purely hinge upon the design of the cars and the sophistication of their controls, or are other factors also involved?

If I could go back in time to visit an era of motor racing just for the fun of it I would choose the 1930s, and not only because of the mighty German Auto Unions and Mercedes Benz. I would also dearly love to have seen the Alfa Romeos of Scuderia Ferrari and the Maseratis, Bugatti's and Talbots of that period at Spa, Rheims or on the Nurburgring.

In the 1930s, and in the period immediately after the war, each passing year saw exciting new designs of racing cars on the circuits of Europe, and there was real artistry in the lines of the Italian cars in particular, whether or not they could stay with the Silver Arrows. Those were serious times, with the rise of Hitler's Germany and Mussolini's Italy and the ever increasing threat of war which overshadowed the last Grand Prix to be held at Donington Park. Yet in motor racing what is serious can also be fun, as a chat with Manfred von Brauchitsch on the subject would quickly demonstrate. Manfred enjoyed his racing cars in spite of the fact that handling them on the rough

Brian Lister and Graham Whitehead winning the Whitsun Trophy race at Goodwood, in a Lister-Jaguar, in 1958.

roads for hours on end made his hands raw. He revelled in their narrow tyres and inadequate brakes. He relished the adrenaline rush he experienced when tackling the extreme dangers of narrow tree-lined circuits, equipped with only a thin leather helmet, and with vast the quantities of highly inflammable fuel at his back.

Yet motor racing was also fun in more recent times when, for example, Brian Lister, with comparatively modest resources, was able to build a small number of Jaguar-engined cars, unique with their "nobbly" bodywork, painted deep green and bright yellow, and beat the larger works teams with them. It was fun when his cars were driven by the legendry Archie Scott-Brown, who persuaded the governing body to let him race even though he only had one complete and fully useable arm. Brian Lister gave me a pewter model of a 1957 car which was driven exclusively by Archie Scott-Brown in their most successful season. He wrote of *"the great days and memories of the halcyon days of motor sport."*

Motor racing was fun when Ken Tyrrell was able to acquire a Ford Cosworth engine, a top designer, sponsorship from a petrol company and the services of a Jackie Stewart to produce a world beater.

It was fun when two drivers in the same team remained good friends and buddies instead of regarding each other as arch rivals; when there was a spirit of comradeship right across the starting grid, and when all the drivers would gather round a slot car racing circuit and compete against each other with friendly rivalry.

It was fun when the cars themselves possessed real character and didn't look like clones.

Dan Gurney told me that the car he enjoyed driving most was the winning car and that a win seemed to make any car look terrific. I can see his point. The front-engined Aston Martin DBR4/250, which was unveiled in 1959 was a good looking car but, arriving too late to make its mark, is remembered by few now. At the same time the open-wheeled version of the W196 Mercedes Benz was not a pretty car in my estimation, but it was redeemed by the success it achieved in the hands of Juan Fangio and Stirling Moss.

Juan Fangio and some of the cars he drove.

Louis Stanley, who ironically was one of the first to have his cars finished in the colours of a major sponsor, regretted the extent to which big money had come to dominate the sport. He wrote:

> *"Sadly the mega business of Ecclestone and his colleagues has killed the old camaraderie among entrants and drivers. Even more regrettable is the decline in the sense of caring. Everything has become self centred and selfish, everybody has a price. What happens to the other fellow, outside of a limited, self governing elite, is of little consequence."*

I believe that the tide of change in motor racing was too strong for anyone to have been able to resist, and that the sport has been more secure in Bernie Ecclestone's hands than it would have been in those of anyone else who might have taken his place. Modern Formula One owes a great deal to Bernie Ecclestone for his business acumen and to Max Mosley for his legal expertise.

Yet the way things used to be years ago often seems extraordinary to us today. I am thinking, for example, of how in the late 1940s Reg Parnell, having thoroughly enjoyed racing behind another car for many laps while attempting to overtake it, chose to slow down when his opponent slid wide at a bend to give him time to retake the lead, before setting out to beat him "fair and square".

Then again there was the time when Baron Huschke von Hanstein was invited to drive a B.M.W. in the 1940 Mille Miglia with Johnny Lurani. At the last minute Baumer was substituted for Lurani and, as a result, Hanstein was ordered to stay at the wheel for the entire race because of the other's inexperience. Hanstein drove most of the one thousand miles himself but then, sportingly, handed over to his co driver so that he could have the honour of crossing the finishing line to take the chequered flag.

When I wrote to Trevor Taylor, who was of course Jim Clark's team mate in the Lotus team, it was 1993 and he was about to have surgery on his neck. He said that he was paying the price for the accidents he had in his motor racing career, and added that motor racing had become big business and that there was none of the camaraderie that existed in his day.

Signed photograph of Trevor Taylor, with Jim Clark.

TREVOR TAYLOR:
Yorkshire grit personified.

I would agree that in more recent years the "serious versus fun equation" in motor racing has taken a marked shift in the more serious direction. But Eddie Irvine and Eddie Jordan, for example, seemed to have had a sense of fun as well developed as anyone, as also had Ken Tyrrell.

The era of motor racing that belonged jointly to Damon Hill and Michael Schumacher witnessed some races which were as exciting as any others before or since, and Damon's refusal to complain or protest when his opponent's Ferrari swung across the track and damaged his

Williams causing him to lose the race and the World Championship, stands up against any previous example of good sportsmanship.

Damon Hill winning the Spanish Grand Prix in his Williams Renault in 1994.

At the beginning of this book I mentioned Murray Walker's view that no motor race is ever boring. For me, races will always be exciting, and this will be the case especially if a British driver is at or near the front, whether it be a Jensen Button or a Lewis Hamilton.

There have been countless intensely interesting and utterly absorbing episodes in motor racing down through the years. One in particular that springs instantly to my mind is when Lord Hesketh provided a seat for James Hunt in a car which bore his own name and, patriotically painted red, white and blue, won the first Grand Prix for a driver who would go on to become a World Champion.

An important ingredient in motor racing in my opinion is that Ferraris, called by Tony Vandervell "those bloody red cars" should be at or near the front, and if a Nigel Mansell happens to be driving one of them, or if a Lewis Hamilton is challenging them in a McLaren, I can have no complaints. On the other hand, whatever one's nationality, no one could be too chauvinistic to admire the skill of a Juan Fangio, Ayrton Senna or Michael Schumacher.

One ought to spare a thought for all the unwanted attention that motor racing drivers who are internationally known celebrities inevitably receive.

I was given a brief insight into what this must feel like some years ago when I was standing in a queue to buy some ice cream at Hengistbury Head in Dorset. The man in the van thought he recognised me as someone who was well known either on the stage or the screen and, looking over the heads of the dozen or so who stood in the queue between us he made the following comments in between attending to his customers. "How are you then?" "How do you like it here in Bournemouth?" And finally rather uncertainly, "It is you isn't it?" In the end I tried to spare his embarrassment by saying, "It's alright, everybody thinks I'm Val Doonican until I start to sing!" Needless to say there is no resemblance, and I have no idea for whom he actually mistook me, yet

I noticed that the people in the queue regarded me with an element of interest as though I had gained a degree of celebrity merely by association!

Famous motor racing drivers are constantly surrounded by fans at race meetings and they are spotted by enthusiasts in shops and elsewhere. But I have never come across one who was not friendly and good humoured and, whether it has only amounted to a brief passing acquaintance or to a lasting friendship, I value those I have come to know over the years as an enthusiast who happens also to enjoy painting motor racing subjects.

In the days when Graham Hill drove a Gold Leaf Lotus, his sponsor arranged a celebration of his one hundredth Grand Prix. When he rose to reply to all the plaudits he had received from the previous speakers Graham lit a Players Gold Leaf and started to cough. He continued to cough until he found the breath to say with a straight face, "That's the end of the commercial!"

I owe that story to Sir Jackie Stewart and I would like to offer the last word on the subject of this book to him. When asked if, having retired many years before, he would risk it all again if he could go back, Jackie said that he would love to have had Jimmy Clark, Graham Hill and Francois Cevert alongside him but that, apart from that, it had been a good life.

While remembering those and many others who won fame on the racing circuits and who are no longer with us, motor racing has been an absorbing entertainment and a fascinating interest for me as an enthusiastic observer, It has been great fun, and the means of getting to know some of the greatest people one could ever wish to meet.

Johnny Dumfries creating a shower of sparks in his Lotus Renualt in 1986.

B. G. Apps '96.

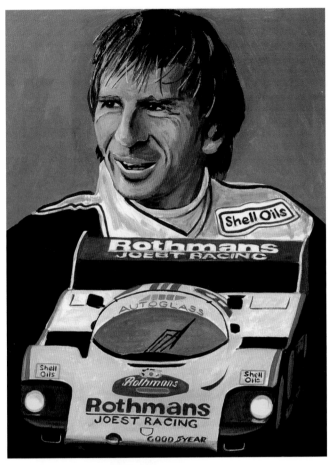

Derek Bell with his Le Mans
winning Porsche 962C in 1986.

Johnny Herbert and the
Benetton Renault in 1995.

David Coulthard and the
Williams Renault in 1994.

Lewis Hamilton – World Champion 2008.